More Praise for
*How to Get Straight A's in School
and Have Fun at the Same Time*

"My three children benefited by Gordon Green's earlier book for college students—now I'm telling them to get this one for their kids!"

—Michael Novak
Syndicated columnist, author
and former U.S. Ambassador

"Having worked as a professional educator for over thirty years, it was very refreshing to read Dr. Gordon Green's book. His formula for student success is simple but very effective. His universal message to the students includes all of the necessary ingredients for them to succeed in school: believe in yourself, be properly prepared, set appropriate and attainable goals, and accomplish them. His book is a wonderful guide about how to combine having fun and getting straight 'A's.' "

—Donald J. Weinheimer Jr., Ed. D.
Principal, Fairfax High School
Fairfax, Virginia

"Dr. Green provides a great service for student athletes of all ages. At our overnight baseball camps, held at Mount St. Mary's College, Doc Green is one of our feature speakers.

Our evening mandatory 'chalk talk of the week' features Doc Green relating his tried and true methods on How to Get Straight A's. His lecture is of great benefit to our school and is well received by the baseball campers from ages eight through eighteen."

—Chuck Faris
Faris Baseball School

"I wish I had this wonderful book when I was in school. Now I hope that my students will get it and take Gordon Green's practical, easy to apply, and always on the mark advice. What else can I say?"

—Douglas J. Besharov
Resident Scholar
American Enterprise Institute
and Professor
Maryland School for Public Affairs

"What Gordon Green says he'll deliver—he delivers! I wish I had this book when I was in school a hundred years ago."

—Ben Wattenberg
Host, PBS's "Think Tank"
and Senior Fellow
American Enterprise Institute
Washington DC

"I have just finished reading the most wonderful book by Dr. Green. Dr. Green presents a road map for students (and parents) on how to maximize their efforts to achieve the best they can. I regret that such a book wasn't available when I was sometimes struggling through term papers and tests and homework. I am so impressed with this book that I have given it to a friend for use by her children. This book should be available to all."

—Lavan Dukes
Educational Policy Director
Florida Department of Education

"For years I worked with underachieving secondary school and college students. That work convinced me that the cause of student underachievement is not the lack of ability, but rather the lack of the right tools. Dr. Green's book is a 'tool box' that provided guidance for use of a variety of effective learning tools. Acquiring even one of these tools will increase a student's chance for academic success."

—Dori Nielson, Ed.D.
Director of Measurement and
Accountability
Montana Office of Public Instruction

"Here it is! All in one place. Read this book and your grades have got to improve!"

—Andy Rogers
Director, ITD
Los Angeles Unified School District

How to Get Straight

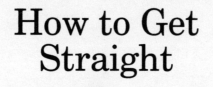
A's

in School
and Have Fun
at the Same Time

Plus:

How to Read a Book
How to Take a Test
How to Write a Paper

GORDON W. GREEN, JR., Ph.D.

FORGE®

A Tom Doherty Associates Book • New York

HOW TO GET STRAIGHT A's IN SCHOOL AND
HAVE FUN AT THE SAME TIME

This book is printed on acid-free paper.

Designed by Lisa Pifher

A Forge Book
Published by Tom Doherty Associates, LLC
175 Fifth Avenue
New York, NY 10010

Forge® is a registered trademark of Tom Doherty Associates, LLC

Library of Congress Cataloging-in-Publication Data
Green, Gordon W.
     How to get straight A's in school and have fun at the same time:
plus: how to read a book, how to take a test, how to write a paper /
Gordon W. Green, Jr.—1st ed.
          p.   cm.
     "A Tom Doherty Associates book."—T.p. verso.
     ISBN 0-312-86659-3 (alk. paper)
     1. Study skills Handbooks, manuals, etc. 2. Test-taking skills
Handbooks, manuals, etc. 3. Report writing Handbooks, manuals,
etc. 4. School children Handbooks, manuals, etc. I. Title.
  LB1601.G73   1999
  371.3'028'1—dc21   99-23091
                                                                    CIP

Printed in the United States of America

0 9 8 7 6 5

For all students, now and in the future, so they can fly through the air like eagles rather than walk on the ground like turkeys.

Contents

Foreword   9
Acknowledgments   13
Introduction   15

PART 1.
The Skills You Need to Learn

1.   How to Read a Book   31
2.   How to Take a Test   47
3.   How to Write a Paper   83

PART 2.
How to Make Straight A's

1.   Take the Right Subjects   111
2.   Work with Your Teacher   119
3.   Never Miss a Class   125
4.   Always Sit Up Front   133
5.   Complete Your Homework Before Class   139
6.   Take Notes During Class   149
7.   Review Your Notes Before the Next Class   159
8.   Prepare for Tests Ahead of Time   167
9.   Be Testwise and Confident   179
10.   Show What You Know on the Final Exam   189

PART 3.
Making It Work for You

1. Develop Good Study
   Habits   199
2. Conclusion   211

   About the Author   219
   Index   221

Foreword

(. . . let's begin at the beginning.)

"Get straight A's? *ME?*"

That may be what you are thinking right now. It's a very natural response, especially if you have not made many A's in the past. It is something that every student would like to do, but it may seem more like a dream than something that could really happen.

Your next question will probably be, "What do I have to do to make straight A's? Will I have to spend the rest of my life indoors, using all of my time reading books and working problems?"

The answer to that question is, *absolutely not!* The most important thing you will need is a knowledge of how to make straight A's, so you can spend your time wisely and still have time left over to do all of the other things you want to do. Now, I don't want to

mislead you and make you think you will not have to
work hard to get straight A's, because you surely will.
The main difference is that you will be working
smarter, not just harder!

Let me give you an example. If you were a jeweler
whose job it was to split diamonds, you would have to
know exactly what tools to use, how to use your tools,
and where to strike the diamond to get the best result.
Striking the diamond just to split it would probably de-
stroy it completely. In the same way, knowing what to
do in school and how to apply what you learn is much
more important than spending a lot of your time studying in the wrong direction.

If you know what you are doing, you can be at the
top of the class in all of your subjects. You can enjoy
studying for a test and be confident that you will do
well on it. You can even enjoy taking the test because
it is an opportunity to show just how much you know
about the subject. And most of all, you will enjoy
bringing home the high marks that will impress your
friends, teachers, parents, and maybe even yourself!
That's what this book is all about. I am going to show
you how to do all of these things.

Still wondering whether it can happen for you? Well,
here's a little proof that it has already happened for others. On the next page you will find the seventh-grade
report card for my son, Chris Green, from the Lanier
Middle School in Fairfax, Virginia. You can be sure this
perfect record was not luck, because in the eighth grade
Chris did the same thing—straight A's in every course,
every quarter for the entire school year. In fact, the
school gave Chris a special award, called the Brad

SIDNEY LANIER MIDDLE SCHOOL

Fairfax County Public Schools

CERTIFICATE OF RECOGNITION

This certifies that

CHRIS GREEN

has been awarded this certificate for

All A Honor Roll for the Entire 1996/97 School Year

Date June 18, 1997

SPONSOR

PRINCIPAL

MIDDLE SCHOOL PROGRESS REPORT

REPORT OF

(501) SIDNEY LANIER MIDDLE SCHOOL

	HOME	GRADE	STUDENT ID	PERIOD ENDS
GREEN, CHRISTOPHER GORDON	0121	07	737207	06/18/97

SUBJECT	TEACHER	1	2	SEM	3	4	FINAL EXAM	FINAL MARK	CLASS ABSENCES	COMMENTS				CONF REQ	INT REPT SENT
KEYBD & TECH	SIEGEL				A	A	A	A	0						*
INTRO FOREIGN LAN	JOUBIN	A	A		A	A		A	0						
EXP WHEEL C	CICHOCKI	A	A			A		A	0						*
U S HISTORY 7	MUNDT	A	A		A	A		A	0						
LUNCH/ADVISORY	WILLIAMS								0						
MATHEMATICS 7	MEHAL	A	A		A	A		A	0	1	2				*
HEALTH & PE 7	CHISHOLM	A	A		A	A		A	1						
ENGLISH 7 GT	FITZHUGH	A	A		A	A	A	A	0						*
SCIENCE 7 GT	WILLIAMS	A	A		A	A	A	A	0						*

	DAYS ON ROLL	ABSENT	PRESENT
	182	1	181

SIGNATURE OF PARENT OR GUARDIAN

SEE REVERSE SIDE FOR
INTERPRETATION OF
MARKS AND COMMENTS.

Fiedler NJHS Award, for making straight A's during his entire time at the school.

Chris is an excellent student, but he doesn't spend all of his time studying. In fact, he plays baseball in several leagues. If he can do it, so can you!

I'm holding a spot for you in the next printing of this book. All you have to do is send me your report card with a perfect record like this one, and I will publish it. It will be a great inspiration for other students who will realize that it can also happen for them.

Gordon W. Green, Jr., Ph.D.

Acknowledgments

(. . . let's give credit where credit is due.)

Several individuals played important roles in the development of this book. First and foremost, I would like to thank my literary agent, Harold Roth, who has guided my efforts over the years and has always given me good advice. He is one of the smartest persons I have ever known, and he always takes a genuine interest in my work and helps to make it better. Without his influence, I wouldn't even be in this business.

My interactions with people in the educational community have helped me enormously. I want to thank the many teachers I have had all through school, who helped shape my life and showed me that education is one of the most valuable things in the world. One who stands out above all the rest is Sheldon Haber, my Ph.D. advisor at The George Washington University. I have also learned much from the many students I have worked with over the years.

I received a lot of valuable assistance from people at my publishing house, Tom Doherty Associates, Inc. My editor for this book, Kathleen Doherty, is certainly the most accomplished editor I have ever encountered. She gave me many significant suggestions that resulted in a better product, and made me sound much better than I really am. Other individuals who provided valuable editorial assistance are Jonathan Schmidt and Barbara Aria.

And then, of course, there is family. I have learned much from my three children, Heidi, Dana, and Christopher, as they have made their way through school and shared their experiences with me. My own parents, Gordon and Marie Green, taught me many of the techniques presented here, and certainly have had a profound influence on my own intellectual development. And last but not least, I would like to recognize my wife, Maureen Green, who gives me encouragement and helps me out with my family responsibilities when I am involved in a project such as this one.

Introduction

(. . . are you ready to get started?)

When the students were asked to make their selection for "Most Likely to Succeed" in the school yearbook, a boy named Gary was everybody's choice. Gary always seems to have everything going in his direction. In all of his classes, Gary is the first to raise his hand when the teacher asks a question, the one who always gets the highest grades on tests and papers, and a straight-A student who makes the honor roll every semester.

Gary's success is not limited to his studies. He is a star athlete who plays baseball in the spring, tennis in the summer, football in the fall, and basketball in the winter. In addition to his studies, Gary participates in many school activities such as the math, science, and photography clubs. He is also the class president, and a member of the honor society.

With such a busy schedule, you might think that Gary is always in a hurry or a nervous wreck—perhaps someone who does not have any time for rest and relaxation, or just having fun with his friends. Such is not the case. In between classes you will see Gary chatting with his many friends, and when someone asks him to attend a party, go to the movies, or do something else, he always seems to have time. He even seems to be in control of the little things, such as keeping up with the latest fads or wearing the latest fashions.

How does Gary do it all? That is the question asked by Gary's friends, and even by his parents and teachers. Some of his friends think he is a genius, someone who masters everything naturally without having to put in all of the hard work required of others. Others think he is an overachiever who is under tremendous pressure but just hides it very well.

None of these theories is correct. Gary does have a secret for his success—it is the formula that he uses in class, on the athletic field, and in his many other activities. Put very simply, Gary believes in himself, takes things seriously, works hard, and knows what he is doing. We can all learn a lot from Gary!

This is a book about becoming a better student in school, but I am going to make some comparisons between school and athletics because they have so many similarities. When I talk to many students they tell me that they enjoy playing sports more than they enjoy going to school. Some even describe school as work and sports as play. Now, I will admit that there are some important differences between the two. The point is that the same skills will help you excel in school and in sports, and school can be fun too!

In order to become a top student or athlete you have to believe in yourself. If athletes go into a game thinking that they will lose, then they probably will. If students go into a test thinking that they will fail, then they probably will. This is called the "self-fulfilling prophecy." What it means is that you usually will do as well as you think you will do. If you do not have confidence in yourself, then you will not be able to perform at your best level. Also, if you do not have confidence in yourself, do not expect others—like teachers or coaches—to have confidence in you, either.

You will find that all top students and athletes take their activities seriously. They believe in what they are doing, and work their hardest to be the very best they can. For athletes, this means attending all of the practices, and playing as if they were actually in a game. The more balls a baseball or softball player hits, the more baskets a basketball player shoots, and the more serves a tennis player makes, the better they will play in a game. For you, the student, this means attending all of your classes, and doing your assignments as if they were tests. The more math and science problems you solve, the more English papers you write, the better you will do on a test.

There is one more comparison that I want to make between school and sports, and it is probably the most important thing I am going to tell you. It's not enough to work hard. In order to succeed, you have to know what to work hard *at*. Think about it for a minute—

that's why you have a coach in sports. A good coach does not just tell a baseball or softball player to get a hit, a basketball player to make a basket, or a tennis player to serve an ace. A good coach teaches players the "body mechanics"—or the most efficient ways to use their bodies—so they will know how to play their sport properly.

When you go to school you have plenty of teachers to instruct you in subjects such as science, history, English, and math, but who teaches you the proper way to study and take tests? Most schools do not have coaches to teach students these skills, which is unfortunate. Knowing how to study and take tests does not come naturally for everyone. In fact, it does not come naturally for most. But I want to tell you right now that you can learn how to study and you can learn how to take tests. I want to be your coach at school to teach you the right way—which is really what this book is all about.

Since I am going to be your coach at school, I should tell you a little bit about myself. I have my doctor's degree (Ph.D.) in economics, and I work for the federal government at the U.S. Census Bureau. My office collects a lot of information on a lot of different subjects, including elementary school, middle school, high school, and college. Several years ago I wrote a book called *Getting Straight A's*, which was mainly for college students. This book gave instructions on the proper way to read books, take tests, and write papers, and it presented a system for making A's in college. It was based on the methods *I* used to make straight A's—and when I was studying economics in graduate school, I made an A not only in every course but also on every test. That will give you an idea of how well my study methods work!

Hundreds of thousands of students have used my study methods, and many have told me about their success. Some have even sent me their report cards to show me how much better they are doing in their studies since they started using my system. Another thing I do is travel around to schools and talk to students and athletes about how they can do better in school. In this book, *How to Get Straight A's in School and Have Fun at the Same Time*, I am doing the same thing for students such as yourself. You are never too young to become a good student, because if you learn the right study habits now, you can use them for the rest of your life.

Let me tell you about some of the things I am going to cover in this book. Even though we are all using computers more and more, reading books is still the most important way we learn information. Most people think that the way to read a book is just to start at the first page and work your way through to the last page, but that is wrong. There are certain things you should do first, such as looking at the headings and summaries so you will understand more as you actually read the book. There are also certain questions you should be asking yourself, which will help you understand what the author is trying to tell you. These are just some of the things you will be learning in the chapter on "How to Read a Book."

Most students think tests are the most unpleasant part of going to school. And yet, you have to face up to the fact that you are going to be taking lots of tests while you are in school, at all grade levels. What you need to know is that there are certain skills for taking tests and getting good grades. In the chapter on "How to Take a

Test," you will learn what to do before you start the test, the best order to answer the questions, and the best way to answer the questions. I am going to cover all different types of tests, such as essays, true-false, multiple choice, and so on. Once you learn these skills you will not only do better on tests, you may even start enjoying taking them.

No matter what class you are taking, you will probably have to write some type of paper, essay, or report. Good writing is something that you can learn, just like almost anything else in life. In the section on "How to Write a Paper," I will teach you some valuable skills that will help you write a better paper or report. I will show you how to pick the best subject to write about, how to research books and other sources, how to prepare an outline, how to write a first draft, and how to put it all together in an excellent paper. I will also be telling you what to do at each step, so you will have plenty of time to finish everything and be happy with your work.

These are the basic skills I will be teaching you, but there is a whole lot more. If you are going to succeed in school, you need to know what you should be doing at home to prepare for lessons, how to learn everything you can in class, and how to get ready for tests. You will also need to know how to get everything done on schedule, so there is plenty of time left to do all of the other things you want to do, such as playing sports or just goofing off. These are the things that my study system is all about.

The first thing you need to do is set some goals for yourself, so you know what you are trying to accomplish. I will help you think about the kinds of subjects you should take in school, so you can get the job you want when you get out of school. I think you will see why school is so important, and how it can affect the rest of your life.

I am also going to cover a lot of things you can do in the classroom to become a better student. Your teacher is very important to your success, and I am going to show you how to make a good impression and get along better with your teacher. You will understand why it is so important not to miss classes if you want to do well. And, believe it or not, you will see that it is easier to learn when you are sitting in certain places in the classroom.

One of the best ways to succeed at anything in life is to be prepared, and this is especially true in school. I will show you how to prepare by doing homework assignments the right way, so you will know something about the lesson before the teacher discusses it in class. I will also show you how to understand everything the teacher says in class, and how to remember it later for a test.

Not only must you know the skills for taking tests, you must also prepare for them ahead of time. I will show you how to know when to start studying for a test, and exactly what to study so you will do well on the test. The students who do the best on tests usually figure out ahead of time what questions the teacher is likely to ask, and this is another thing I will be teaching you. When you are well prepared, taking tests can actually be fun because you will want to show the teacher how much you have learned.

One of the most important ways to become a good student is to have good study habits. If you have good study habits then everything will come easily and naturally; if you have bad study habits then everything will be a struggle. I will be giving you a lot of tips on when to study, where to study, what to study, and how to study. Once you develop these habits, you will find that studying is as simple and painless as brushing your teeth every day.

Even after I—your coach—give you all of this knowledge, you must understand that it is still up to *you* to carry everything out. I do not want you to think that you can become an excellent student without a lot of hard work. You have to work hard to become good at anything in life, and in this respect school is a lot like sports. You can know everything about a sport, but you will not become really good unless you practice and work hard. The difference with my system of study is that you will be working smarter, not just harder.

What are you going to get for all of this hard work? I know that your parents, relatives, and teachers have all talked to you many times about the importance of doing well in school. And I know that sometimes, at a young age, it is difficult to understand the importance of what they are saying. Therefore, I want you to listen to it one more time from your coach!

I have been around for a long time, and I have spent much of my life trying to understand what people do to enjoy their work and be successful at it. Here is what I have found: If you have a good education you can go into almost any type of work that you want. But it is important to understand that you need to have certain types of training to do certain types of jobs. For example, if you want to be a doctor, not only do you have to go to college, you also have to go to medical school and become an intern before you can become a doctor. There is no other way to do it! The other thing that you should understand is that you need to have good grades all through school if you are going to get into a good college and get a good job.

The next time that your parents or someone else tells you that you need to make good grades, just remember that you are doing it for *you,* not for them. They are looking out for you, but you are the one who has to live the rest of your life. If you want to have the freedom to do the type of work you want later on, and make plenty of money, then you need to take school seriously now!

There is no better time to begin than right now, and your coach is anxious to get you out on the academic playing field to make you a star student. But first, you need a little training. Are you ready to begin? Just remember:

RECAP

To become the best student in class, you must:

1. **believe in yourself,**

2. **take school seriously and work hard,**

3. **know what you are doing.**

1

The Skills You Need to Learn

(. . . to become a straight-A student.)

WHAT YOU WILL LEARN

Every activity requires you to have certain skills to be effective. You need to have certain skills to play different types of sports, or you will never develop to your full ability. For example, a baseball player must know how to field, throw, and hit a baseball; a basketball player needs to know how to dribble, pass, and shoot a basketball; and a football player must be skilled at passing, running, and kicking a football.

Becoming a top student is no exception—certain skills are required here, too! To become a top student you must be able to understand information from reading assignments, demonstrate that you have mastered this information in a variety of tests, and prepare well-written essays and papers. Without these basic skills, you will never develop your full ability as a student. To help you develop these skills, this section contains three chapters: "How to Read a Book," "How to Take a Test," and "How to Write a Paper."

Your first thought may be, "Is all of this really necessary?" After all, as you've progressed through school you have probably read a number of books, taken more tests than you care to remember, and written enough papers to fill a small library. Shouldn't all of this experience have helped you to develop these skills, in the same way that an athlete practicing his or her sport gets better over time?

The answer to this question is both "yes" and "no." There is no doubt that doing something over and over again will improve your ability, whether it involves sports or school. But the important point is that if you do not learn the *proper* way to do something, you will spend more time than necessary and never be as good as you might have become. In fact, when we have done something the wrong way for too long, we have to put extra effort into unlearning it so we can move to a higher level.

There is a lot more to mastering the basic study skills than you might at first think. You should not think that you are going to understand everything in a book just because you have read it from cover to cover, or that you will make an A on every test just because you have studied very hard, or that you will write an excellent paper just because you have done a lot of research and put a lot of effort into writing it. What counts is not only the amount of effort that you put into something, but how you went about it!

In this section, I am going to teach you the basic

skills that I have developed over the years, which have helped me and numerous others become better students. I will show you how to become an active reader so you can understand your reading assignments in the shortest time. I am going to teach you the skills you need to score as high as you are able on different types of tests, such as essay exams, objective exams, problem exams, open-book exams, take-home exams, and oral exams and reports. Finally, I am going to show you how to write an interesting and excellent paper that will also be fun to write.

After you learn these basic skills, I will show you in the next section how to use them to become a straight-A student.

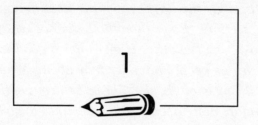

How to Read a Book

(. . . and understand everything in it.)

When you see Sally she is usually carrying a book under her arm. I am not talking only about the times when you see Sally at school. She often has a book with her when she is at the shopping mall, riding in the car, going to see relatives, or doing just about anything where there might be an opportunity to read. Now, you might think Sally is a bookworm, but that would not be accurate because she enjoys spending a lot of time with her friends and doing a lot of different things. Very simply put, books are one of Sally's main hobbies.

People practice their hobbies in many different ways. Some people like to collect stamps or trading cards, others like to listen to music or go to the movies, and still others like to travel and visit new places. Sally likes to read books—all different kinds of books. She is happy to browse through the library looking at different titles in different sections. Even though she is not reading all of these books, she feels that it gives her a good idea of the various things people have written about. When her interest is strong enough, she takes a book out of the library to investigate more deeply. She also likes to go to a large bookstore near her home, where she can see the latest releases or perhaps pick up a bargain book for her own library.

Sally's love of books has made it a lot easier for her to do well in school because, after all, you do have to read a lot of books in your classes. When Sally gets an assignment and has to read a chapter, it almost seems like she is practicing her hobby. The books she uses in her classes are written very clearly and are really quite interesting. The only thing that is different is that sometimes she has to do a written exercise for the school assignment. To Sally that seems like a small price to pay for the opportunity to read another book about something new and interesting.

Reading assignments come more easily for Sally than for most other students. First of all, she has read so many books and learned so many new words that the whole experience feels very natural to her. Also, Sally usually only has to do an assigned reading one time because she understands just about everything the first time through. Sally has more fun reading than most students because she really knows how to read a book.

The reason I have told you this story is to suggest that reading books can be fun, and that there are certain methods you can use to get the most out of them. When picking up a book, your first impulse might be to jump right in and start reading from the first page. Unfortunately, this is the wrong way to go about it because you are probably going to miss a lot of information, or have a hard time organizing it. There are several things you need to do first to get the most out of a book. You need to think about what you are doing, and then take a couple of important steps. Like Sally, you need to learn the proper way to read a book.

Before I give you advice on how to read a book, I want to say a few things about what books mean to me. As you might expect, since I am an author, books are very important to me. I like to collect all different types of books, in the same way that many people like to collect other things or follow hobbies. I think I have probably saved every book I have ever had from my earliest years. When I go to book shows, I meet a lot of other authors and they give me autographed copies of their books. I have several bookshelves built into walls in my house to help organize all of these books.

When I walk through my study and look at my books, they give me a special feeling. I can glance at the title of a book, and the main idea of what the book is about immediately comes to my mind. This makes me realize just how much I have learned from all of the books I have read over my lifetime, and how much enjoyment they have given to me. People who write books usually know a lot about a subject, and when they write their thoughts down they have to think very deeply and express themselves very clearly. You probably know from your own experiences that it takes a lot of effort to write some-thing that is worth reading.

There is another point I want to make about books, and it is one that most of us take for granted: Books give us the opportunity to learn about the ideas of great thinkers, even those who have been dead many years. When we read their words, it is almost as if they are sitting in the room right next to us. Without books we could only learn about their ideas through the interpre-tations of others. If you think about it, you will realize that books are the means by which knowledge has been transmitted across the ages.

Even more important to you, the books you read in school will help you learn more about the subject you are studying and score higher on tests. Teachers will often ask you to do a reading assignment on a subject before they discuss it in the classroom. If you have done your reading ahead of time, you will under-stand more when the teacher presents it in class. So you see, reading and understanding books is essential if you want to do well in school. Given the importance of books, you want to make sure that you get the most out of them.

Getting Ready to Read

Now, let's suppose that you have just picked up a new textbook for one of your classes, and you are going to do your first reading assignment. You may be anxious to jump right in and start reading, but there are a couple of things you should do beforehand.

The first thing to do is find a spot where you will be able to read in comfort—remember, reading should be a leisurely activity. I like to wear very loose, comfortable clothing, and find a big easy chair where I can relax. You don't want to get too comfortable, however, or you might find yourself dozing off. Some people feel very relaxed reading at their desks, particularly if they are studying math and science and need to write something down. This is really a personal matter, and you will need to decide on the spot that works best for you.

Your reading spot should also be quiet enough so you will not be distracted by other noises in the house.

You will find it easier to read if your reading spot has plenty of light. If you read in a dark corner, you may get tired or even damage your eyes. I find that I stay more alert by reading under fluorescent light than a bright lamp. Try to sit where the light will shine overhead, or over your shoulder, rather than in your eyes.

Now that we have all of that out of the way, let's talk about how to read that new textbook.

Review Before Reading

When you get a new textbook, it is always a good idea to look the book over before actually starting to read it. The complete title on the first page, or title page, will give you a good idea of what the book is about. You should read the short statement about the author at the back of the book to learn something about the author's background and experiences. Next, read the preface or introduction at the beginning of the book to find out why the author wrote the book, and what he or she hopes to accomplish. Following this, look over the table of contents to see the specific subjects that are covered and how they are organized. This approach will give you a good overall idea of what the book is about.

You still need to do that reading assignment that the teacher handed out. Do you just go to the first page and start reading? Not yet—it's still too soon. You should get an overall idea of what the reading assignment is about before actually reading it.

Let's say that the reading assignment is the first chapter in the book. You should quickly flip through all of the pages in the first chapter to see what it contains and how it is organized. As you flip through, look at the major headings, minor headings, summary statements, and conclusions. Pay particular attention to anything in bold print, or any graphs, pictures, or equations in the chapter.

By skimming through the chapter in this manner, you have obtained a good idea of how it is organized and what it contains. You have just sent a lot of information to your mind, so you will understand and remember more when you start reading the chapter. This is because you will have an idea of what is coming next, how it fits in with what you have already read, and how everything fits together to tell the whole story. Always preview your reading assignments in this way before actually reading them.

Now you're ready to actually start reading the assignment. If you are wondering whether you just start at the beginning and read all of the way to the end, you need to know that there is a whole lot more to it than that. *How* you read the book will determine *how much* you get out of, it!

Ask Questions as You Read

The main thing to remember in reading a book is that you need to be an "active" reader, not a "passive" reader. Do you know the difference between the two, and which description applies to you?

A passive reader may read all of the words, but does not think or concentrate deeply about what they mean. This type of reader does not try to figure out what the author is trying to say, does not relate one sentence or thought to another, and does not compare the ideas to his or her own experiences. Passive readers do not ask any questions—they are just trying to get the assignment done so they can go on to something else they would rather be doing. As a result, their attention starts to drift, and they find themselves thinking about anything other than what they are reading—such as, what am I going to do after school with my friends? Who's going to win the ball game tonight? I wonder if that movie I am going to see is any good? Passive readers don't enjoy what they read, and they sure don't get much out of it, either.

The active reader will have a much better understanding of what a book is about, and will find the experience very enjoyable. Active readers not only understand each idea presented by the author, they also understand the relationships between the ideas. Understanding is not the same as memorizing, because you can memorize something without understanding it. If you really understand something, you can describe it in your own words and it will mean the same thing that the author said.

The way to reach a high level of understanding about what an author is saying is to ask yourself some important questions while you are reading the book, *and* try to answer them. For example, you should ask yourself (1) what the book is all about, (2) what it says in detail, and (3) whether the author has said something similar to what your teacher said in class.

The best way to understand what you are reading is to compare it to your own knowledge and experiences. Ask yourself if you have experienced something similar to what you are reading about, or if what you have read changes your view of the world or the way things work. Sometimes this can be difficult, especially if you are reading about something you have not experienced, such as the Vietnam or Gulf Wars. In such cases, you might want to discuss the subject with an adult who has lived through the experience. The important point is that by making these comparisons, it will be easier for you to understand and remember what you have read.

If you want to become a more active reader, you should also ask yourself some critical questions. What do I mean by critical questions? I mean that you should constantly question *what* the author is saying. For example, see if you can figure out what questions the author is trying to answer, and how he or she goes about answering them. Ask yourself what the author has assumed, and whether his or her statements are based on knowledge, facts, experiences, or opinions.

You should also ask yourself if the author is presenting things fairly, and decide whether you agree or disagree with him or her. If you disagree, is it because the author has not explained things clearly, or perhaps not offered any proof for the statements? You may not know the answers to all of these questions, but asking them—and trying to answer them!—will make you a much better reader.

Sometimes it is difficult to keep everything straight in your head, especially if you are reading about a subject that is complicated. You may find it helpful to jot certain things down on paper as you read, such as points that you want to remember, or questions that you want to think more deeply about. The simple act of writing things down helps many people to understand a subject more fully. You are more likely to do this if you have a pencil and paper on hand when you sit down to read.

Good readers ask themselves questions all of the time, even after they have finished reading. For example, after you have finished a chapter, take a few minutes to quiz yourself on the material presented by the author. Ask yourself the question, "What have I really learned in this chapter, and what are the main ideas I am taking away from it?"

In addition to asking yourself questions, there are several other things you can do to become a more active reader. They all involve trying to understand everything of importance that the author has presented in the book.

Use the Dictionary

If you want to understand what the author is trying to tell you, then you must read and understand all of the words he or she uses in the book. For the rest of your life you will be developing your vocabulary. If you come across words that you do not understand, you should take the time to look up their meaning in the dictionary. Sometimes you can understand what a word means by the way it is used in a sentence. This is helpful, but it is not a substitute for looking words up in the dictionary.

In addition to looking up words that you do not know in the dictionary, here is a simple activity that will help build your vocabulary: Each day, glance through the dictionary and find one word that you don't know. Make a point of mastering one new word a day, and by the end of the year you will have mastered 365 new words. It may help if you write down each new word in a notebook along with relevant information about it.

When you look up a word in the dictionary, take a few minutes to study the information provided. In particular, look at the origin of words (where they came from), how to spell and pronounce them, different parts of speech, and their various meanings. Try to associate the word with something or with an experience in your own life, because this will make it easier to remember the word. If you are looking up technical words for a science class, it is very important to understand their meaning, or you will not be able to understand the idea being discussed.

Looking up words in the dictionary will not only help you understand what the author is trying to say, it will also build your vocabulary. As you learn more words it will be easier to understand other authors, and you will be able to express yourself more clearly when writing essays or answers to exam questions. This will help you in all of your classes, not just English. You should never stop looking up words in the dictionary; I still do it today. Just think, the more words you learn, the fewer you will have to look up in the dictionary later on.

Understanding the Author's Message

If you really want to understand everything the author is trying to tell you, then you have to read everything presented in the book. This means that not only do you have to read the words, you must also study and understand all of the charts, graphs, tables, and pictures in the book. Some students skip over these materials, but this is a big mistake. You should realize that the author put them there for a very good reason, and you may be missing something very important if you skip over them. Charts and graphs complement the text. When you take time to understand these visual aids, you gain a better understanding of what you are reading about.

Even if you have read something very carefully, and looked up words in the dictionary, it may be difficult to understand what the author is trying to say. Some subjects are very complicated, so you may have to dig deeper to understand them.

If this is the case, you may have to reread a book in a different way to figure out what the author is trying to say. One approach is to read more slowly and concentrate on one sentence at a time. One of my favorite sayings is "Learn to read slow—all other graces will follow in their proper places." After you read a sentence, stop for a few seconds and ask yourself what the sentence means. Try to relate the new information to what the author has already covered.

Let me give you an example of this approach. Suppose in your history or government textbook you read that the First Amendment is the source of Americans' freedom of religion, speech, press, and assembly. Think carefully about what this means. The author may have already discussed the Bill of Rights, and mentioned that it comprises the first ten amendments to the U.S. Constitution. You may want to refer back to the discussion of the Bill of Rights to compare the First Amendment with the other amendments.

If you still cannot understand what the author is saying, mark the confusing part and skip over it. Read ahead a little bit further and then go back to the part you did not understand; it may now be easier to figure out. Sometimes we can understand ideas by looking at other ideas in a story, in the same way that we can understand words by looking at other words in a sentence.

To become an active reader, you must discover the methods that allow *you* to learn most effectively. None of us are the same, and different people use different faculties for learning information. Some people learn the most through their sense of vision, others rely on their sense of hearing, and still others find that different senses work the best for them. For example, some students like to read silently to themselves, others prefer to read out loud, and some find that their best way to learn information is to write it down.

I have seen some people use a magic marker or pencil while they are reading, to underline words, highlight ideas, and write questions in the margin. (Of course, you shouldn't be marking up books that do not belong to you.) If you think about it, we all use some combination of our senses to learn new material. You need to find the combination that works the best for you.

How will you know that you are becoming a more active reader? It's really quite simple. You are becoming an active reader when you can figure out the author's next thought or statement before you actually read it. This means that you have figured out what the author is trying to say and you have lined up your thoughts with his or hers.

Reading Faster

I also have some things to say about the speed at which you read. I know that everyone wants to read faster because there are a lot of other things they would rather be doing, such as playing sports, watching movies, reading other books, or just goofing off. But it is important to remember that you should never emphasize speed above everything else, because you may end up missing a lot.

A lot of nonsense has been written about speed reading. I have seen advertisements that say they can teach you how to read fast by running your finger down the page. That may be the best way to look someone up in the telephone book, but you are not going to learn very much at that speed. Some even say that they can show you how to read the Bible in a couple of hours using their methods. Forget about all of these gimmicks. Most of the people who emphasize speed are just turning a lot of pages so they can tell their friends how many books they have read, rather than what they have learned from them.

The secret to reading faster, and still understanding what you have read, is to see more words as your eyes move across the page. People who can see a whole word at a time will read faster than people who can only see a letter at a time, and people who can see several words in a phrase at a time will read faster than people who can only see one word at a time. As your eyes move across the page, you occasionally have to stop, so the more words you can see before stopping, the faster you will read.

It should now be obvious why looking up the meaning of words in the dictionary is a good idea. If you have a small vocabulary, you will not be able to read at a smooth and rapid rate. Every time you come across a word that you do not know, you have to stop and try to figure out what it means. It may take you more time in the short run to look up the meaning of the word, but in the long run you will be reading faster because there will not be as many interruptions.

It is also important for you to recognize that some books must be read more slowly than others. If you are reading a light novel, you can usually read it very quickly because you can understand the material as fast as you read it. On the other hand, if you are reading science or math books, you usually have to read them more slowly because the subjects are more complicated. If you hurry on to the next topic without fully understanding the one you are reading, then you are just making things harder for yourself. Fortunately, reading assignments in science and math tend to be shorter than in subjects such as English and history.

As you get more experience in reading, you will read more quickly in a very natural way. Just remember that it is always important to read all of the words the author has written rather than skipping over some of them; otherwise, you may miss part of the author's message. You should never force yourself to read at a faster speed than you can handle naturally, because this can be very unpleasant. It can make you feel uncomfortable or even cause your eyes to get tired. I would advise you not to worry about your reading speed. Read at a rate that allows you to understand all of the material in a comfortable way.

By now you should have a good idea of what it takes to become an active reader. An active reader is like an explorer going out to learn new things. By becoming an active reader you will be turning the reading experience into an exciting adventure. The more things you know, the better you will be able to enjoy new knowledge because you will have a better understanding of how the world works. As I mentioned to you at the beginning of this chapter, I get a special feeling when I look at all of the books on my bookshelves that I have read. That special feeling comes from knowing that I have made the authors' wisdom part of my own.

Well, now that you know what you need to do to become an active reader, you should quickly preview this entire book and read the rest of it using the new methods you have learned.

RECAP

To become an active and effective reader:

1. preview a book before actually reading it,

2. continually ask yourself questions,

3. look up new words in the dictionary,

4. read at your own pace.

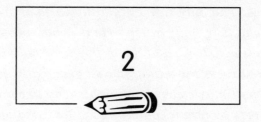

How to Take a Test

(. . . and come out a winner!)

Brett is a baseball player who plays a mean third base. He has kept this position ever since Little League, because of his ability to field almost anything that comes his way. You need quick reflexes to play the "hot corner," and that is exactly what Brett possesses. His teammates have nicknames for him, such as "scoop," the "vacuum cleaner," and "the cat," which describe the way he moves on the field.

Brett faces a tough test. The team they are playing is challenging them for first place in the division, and this is the last game before the playoffs. It has been a tightly played game right up to the last inning, and Brett's team is ahead by only one run. The other team has runners on first and second, and there are two outs. One more out and the game is over, and Brett's team walks away with first place. The only thing standing in their way is the batter, who is a "pull hitter." He is a big, powerful guy who hits line drives right down the third base line.

Brett surveys the situation and gets ready. He knows that the ball may come shooting his way like a rocket. If the ball gets by him it could be good for extra bases, and the other team may get the two runs it needs to win. Brett remembers that his coach said, "Before each pitch, think about what you are going to do with the ball if it comes your way. If you have to think about it after the ball is hit, it may be too late." The last thing that goes through Brett's mind before the pitch is, "All I have to do is touch third base to get the force."

Brett's pitcher delivers the first pitch, and the batter rips a grounder down the third base line. He hits the ball so hard, it looks like it's been shot out of a rifle. Brett's instincts tell him to go horizontal—he dives toward the third base line with his arm outstretched. There is a large puff of dust, and Brett can taste the dirt in his mouth. Through the dusty haze he can see the bright white ball sticking out of the top of his glove like a snow cone. Brett doesn't know the location of the runner on second, but he remembers that all he has to do is touch the bag on third to get the force. Without getting up, Brett moves his outstretched arm and tags third base. The ball game is over, and Brett's team stays in first place.

Brett was tested and he rose to the occasion to help his team to victory. School is not the only place where you are tested. People are tested in just about everything they do, right from the earliest age.

An important lesson is contained in this story. Brett was successful because he prepared ahead of time. Not only did he prepare through all of the hard work he did leading up to the game; he also thought about what he had to do to succeed right before that hard grounder came zooming his way. The same approaches work when taking tests in the classroom, and that is what we will be talking about in this chapter.

The tests you take in school will determine the grades you receive. When you apply for college, your grades will show whether you are a serious student who is likely to succeed. Many colleges require students to take entrance exams to test their general knowledge.

Even though students take many tests, most of them are not very "testwise"—which means that they do not know the skills that will help them score high on tests. The ability to score high on tests is something that can be learned. Even very intelligent and well-prepared students may do poorly on tests if they do not know how to take tests.

In this chapter I am going to teach you the basic skills that will help you score highly on tests. I am going to cover most of the different types of tests that you may have to take at school. For example, I am going to cover the types of tests you have to take in the classroom, such as essay exams (written tests), objective exams (multiple-choice and true-false tests), problem exams (in mathematics and science), and open-book exams (which allow you to use other materials). I am also going to show you the best way to answer take-home exams, and I will say a few words about oral exams and reports.

What to do Before You Take a Test— Get Ready, Get Set . . .

1. Always arrive before an exam begins. Never arrive late! There are two main reasons why you should not be late. First, it might make you nervous and therefore you will not be able to think as well. Second, you may not have as much time to complete the test.

2. Be prepared with supplies that you will need to take the test, such as pencils, pens, erasers, paper, exam books, or any other special equipment such as rulers, compasses, and calculators. If you are prepared, you will not have to worry about how you are going to take the test.

3. Do not listen to your classmates talking about what will be on the test. When you arrive early to take a test, you may overhear your classmates talking about what they think will be on it. You should not listen to any of this discussion. They do not know any more than you do, and their discussion may even lead you in the wrong direction. When you go in to take a test you will have to rely on what you have learned, not on what someone else thinks. If this discussion is bothering you, you can get up and take a little walk to relax.

4. Read and listen to the instructions. Do not jump right into a test without reading or listening to all of the instructions. Think about it for a minute—it is very hard to succeed unless you know what you are supposed to do!

You should listen carefully to the instructions that your teacher gives before the test, and pay particular attention to instructions written on the exam paper.

This is important because the instructions will tell you which questions you have to answer, whether you should answer them in a certain order, what type of answer your teacher expects, and the number of points the teacher will count for each answer. Some students jump right into a test and find out later that they have answered the wrong questions. It is hard enough to make an A on a test even if you answer the right questions!

5. Write your name on the test paper. Wouldn't it be terrible if you worked very hard to make an A on a test, and couldn't even claim it as your own? The teacher might even give your A to someone else.

I am sure that you have heard these basic principles many times before, but it never hurts to hear them again. If you do these things automatically before every test, you will not even have to think about them.

Essay Exams

More and more teachers are giving their students essay (or written) exams these days, even at the lower grade levels. These exams are very popular with teachers because they measure a student's ability to really understand a subject. The teacher can also learn about your thinking behind your answer. In these exams you will not only have to remember information, but also understand and explain it in a very clear way. To write a good answer to an essay exam, you need to be creative in your thinking, organize information effectively, and express it clearly. These are skills that you will need all through your years in school.

Let's suppose that you are taking an essay exam in one of your classes. It might be English, history, science, or whatever. I am going to assume that you have carefully read and listened to the instructions, so you know exactly what you are supposed to do. So now what do you do?

The way you spend the first couple of minutes on the test will determine the questions you answer, how well you answer them, and the grade you receive. It is important to get a good start. I like to use the example of running a race at a track meet. If you get off to a slow start, you may be behind during the whole race and never catch up.

You should use the first couple of minutes to look over the entire exam very carefully. Look at the number of pages in the exam and the number of questions on each page. You should read all of the questions on an essay exam before answering any one of them. There is a danger in trying to answer the questions too quickly, because you may head off in the wrong direction.

As you read each question, ask yourself what is being requested. Does your teacher want to know if you can explain the details, understand the basic principles, or see the relationship between ideas? For an example, let's again consider a question on the First Amendment to the U.S. Constitution. Your teacher may ask you to write the First Amendment (explain the details), tell why it is important (understand the basic principles), or compare it to other amendments (see the relationship between ideas).

Underline the words that tell you what you are supposed to do. Does the question ask you to *discuss* (tell what you know) or *describe* (list the characteristics); to *compare* (list the similarities) or *contrast* (list the differences); to *develop* (draw a conclusion) or *demonstrate* (explain through examples)? These instructions may sound very similar to one another, but each is asking you to do something very different. Think about the exact meaning of the words in the question, so you will be able to figure out the best way to answer it.

If you do not completely understand what a question is asking for, go up and ask the teacher to explain it to you. Don't think that the teacher will be angry about this. Teachers want their students to understand the test questions, so they will have a fair chance at answering them.

As you read each question, write down the words or thoughts that come to mind, because these will be part of your answer. You can write these down in the margin of your test paper or answer sheet. You do not have to write down complete sentences, just words or phrases that will remind you of the thought later, when you answer the question. You should read all of the questions in the exam this way before actually answering any one of them.

There are three good reasons why you should read all of the questions on an essay exam before answering any one of them. First, by reading all of the questions you will know what you have to do on the exam, so you won't be surprised later. Second, sometimes the essay questions are related to each other, and you will want to know this ahead of time. And third, by reading all of the questions at the beginning, you will have more time to think about how to answer the more difficult ones.

Now, let's assume that you have finished reading all of the questions, and are ready to begin answering them. If the teacher has given you a choice of questions, such as three out of four, you have to decide which questions to answer. As you read the questions and wrote down your thoughts, you should have developed a good feel for the ones you know the most about. The common-sense rule is always to select the questions you know the most about. Don't pick the difficult questions just because you are looking for a challenge.

Once you have decided on which questions to answer, quickly add up the point score for them. You should divide up the time available so that you spend a proportionate amount of time on each question based on its point score. For example, suppose you have one hour to answer three questions, one worth fifty points and the other two worth twenty-five each. I would suggest that you allow one-half hour for the fifty-point question and fifteen minutes for each of the twenty-five point questions. You should wear a watch so you will know when to start the second and third questions. Try to stick to this schedule so you will be able to answer all of the questions. It doesn't do any good to do an excellent job on one of the questions, and mess up the other two.

You are just about ready to write an answer to the first question—but which one should you answer first? If the teacher has said that you can answer them in any order you want, always answer the easiest question first and save the more difficult ones until later on. By getting the easier questions out of the way, you will have more confidence when you return to the more difficult ones. This approach will also give you more time—even if it's only a few minutes!—to think about how to put together a good answer for the more difficult questions.

You are now ready to write a complete answer to the first essay question. Let's go through an example that will illustrate in detail the process of how to write an answer. Suppose that the first question you have to answer is the following. (Notice that I have underlined the words that tell what you are supposed to do.)

Describe the First Amendment, and discuss why it is one of the most important amendments to the U.S. Constitution.

When you first read this question at the beginning of the test, you might have jotted down a couple of points that immediately came to mind, such as the following:

1st Amendment—freedom of religion, speech, press, assembly.

Importance—most fundamental personal freedoms.

Now is the time to think more deeply about your knowledge of the subject. Break your knowledge down into different parts, and think about the relationship between these parts. If you come up with different possible answers to the question, throw out all of the answers except the best one—this will be your answer!

As you go through this process, you should be coming up with additional information to include in your answer. Write down this additional information along with the thoughts you wrote earlier. Again, just write down words or short phrases, not complete sentences. For example, you might add to your earlier thoughts in the following manner:

1st Amendment—freedom of religion, speech, press, assembly.

Importance—most fundamental personal freedoms.

Write out 1st Amendment.

Mention Bill of Rights.

Limits powers of central government.

British abuses still in mind.

Uniquely defines being an American.

You should now have all of the major points that will go into your answer. The next step is to organize this information into an answer that will make sense. You don't have time to do an outline, so just number the points in the order you want to present them.

2. 1st Amendment—freedom of religion, speech, press, assembly.

1. Importance—most fundamental personal freedoms.

4. Write out 1st Amendment.

3. Mention Bill of Rights.

6. Limits powers of central government.

5. British abuses still in mind.

7. Uniquely defines being an American.

Now you are ready to begin writing a complete answer to the question. In order to write a good essay, you must make sure that it has a beginning, middle, and end. In the beginning (or introduction) of your essay, you should state your theme very clearly. The theme is the major point or idea in your answer. You will need to develop this theme in the middle (or body) of your essay. Each paragraph should have arguments or reasons that support your theme. As part of your argument, you should mention major facts, ideas, examples, and details. This shows that you have detailed knowledge as well as general knowledge. It also helps to mention some of the things that the teacher said in class, which will show that you have learned some of his or her wisdom. If the essay is for a science class, you should use the right technical terms. Finally, at the end (or conclusion) of the essay, you need to summarize your theme.

As you look at the points you numbered in your outline, points 1 and 2 would make a good introduction, points 3 through 6 could comprise the body, and point 7 would make a good conclusion. Now, let's put it all together to see what the complete essay will look like:

The First Amendment to the U.S. Constitution gives Americans their most fundamental freedoms, including the freedom of religion, speech, press, and assembly.

The First Amendment was part of the Bill of Rights, which comprises the first ten amendments to the U.S. Constitution. The Bill of Rights was passed as a group by the First Congress in 1789, and became part of the U.S. Constitution in 1791.

The First Amendment reads, "Congress shall
make no law respecting an establishment of
religion, or prohibiting the free exercise thereof; or
abridging the freedom of speech, or of the press; or
the right of the people peaceably to assemble, and
to petition the Government for a redress of
grievances."

When the First Amendment was passed, British
abuses of the colonists' civil liberties were still a
recent memory. Newspaper editors and citizens had
been arrested for things they wrote or said, and
were held and forced to confess at gunpoint or
worse. Therefore, the First Amendment restricted the
power of the new central government to violate
these fundamental personal freedoms.

In conclusion, the First Amendment guarantees
our most basic civil liberties, and is what people
often think of when they say that America is the
"land of the free"!

In writing your complete answer, you might have
written out the First Amendment entirely because your
teacher mentioned in class that you were expected to
know it. Therefore, to get the most points for your answer you needed to demonstrate that you knew it by
heart. If there was any doubt, you could have asked the
teacher during the test what he or she expected.

You just had to read several pages about how to answer essay questions. But once you've absorbed the information in these pages, you'll be able to run through
the main points in your mind fairly quickly. It's the same
as if you had to read several pages describing the me-

chanics of how to swing a baseball or softball bat, but it really only takes less than a second to swing it once you know what you are doing.

There is one basic rule that most students do not follow when writing answers to essay questions. The rule is: *Answer only the question that is asked.* Many students write an answer to the question they would *like* to answer rather than the question that is being asked. If you add a lot of extra details and padding, the teacher may think you are trying to fake it because you do not know the real answer. You won't get extra points for unrelated details, and you may even lose points!

Regardless of how much you have studied for an exam, sometimes you will run across questions that you don't immediately know how to answer. Rather than getting frustrated by such questions, you need to accept them as a challenge. If you don't come up with a good answer right away, you need to keep working at it.

We have all come up against questions where, no matter how hard we try, we just cannot come up with a good answer. In such cases, you should at least start to write something. If you have studied for an exam, you must know something that is relevant to the question. As you start to write, think about the major points and general themes you have been studying. Sometimes you will connect with one idea that reminds you of another idea, and perhaps still another idea, until you have a fairly good answer to the question. The one thing you know for certain is that if you do not write anything, you are not going to get any points. If you write something, there is at least a chance that you will get some credit.

Sometimes, no matter how hard you try, you are unable to come up with an answer to an exam question. When this happens, do not spend too much time on the question. Just allow enough space on your test paper for an answer, and move on to the next question. After you have finished with the easy questions, you will be better prepared to answer the more difficult questions because you have had more time to think about them.

The other thing that you need to understand is that you are going to make some mistakes on tests. No one is perfect. Always try to leave some time to review your work so you can correct errors or explain a thought in more detail.

I remember that the most disturbing thing to me was running out of time on a test. You might be working very hard, when suddenly your teacher announces that there are only five minutes left to finish the test. It is even more disturbing when you know the answers to all of the remaining questions, but do not have enough time left to answer them. What should you do in this case?

The most important thing is to stay calm. *Don't panic!* The best thing to do at this point is to write down an outline of how you would have answered the question. You can list the major headings and subheadings, as well as any supporting facts, in a few key phrases. You should also write a short note to your teacher, explaining that you are supplying an outline because you did not have enough time to write a complete answer. In many cases, teachers will give students most of the points for doing this, because they realize that anybody can run out of time. They have probably done it many times themselves.

Objective Exams

"Objective exams" is just a fancy way of referring to tests that include true-false, multiple-choice, fill-in-the-blanks, or matching questions, or some combination of these. The main idea is that everyone has to answer the question in the same way, because there is only one right answer to each question. Some objective exams only test your ability to remember information. Some are more challenging in that they test your ability to understand, interpret, analyze, and apply your knowledge.

Many teachers like to give objective exams all the way through elementary, middle, and high school. They like them because the same standards apply to everyone, and they are easy to grade. The teacher can often get the results back to you in a day or so, and sometimes teachers even have classmates grade them immediately after the test. Because of the importance of these exams, you need to know the best way to take them.

The way to take an objective exam is different from the way you take an essay exam. You should still look over the test to see the number of pages and questions, but you do not need to read through all of the questions before marking your answers. You should answer the questions in the order they appear on the exam. If you come across a difficult question, leave it blank, put a question mark in the margin, and move on to the next question. You can always come back to the difficult questions later on, and they may be easier because you have had more time to think about them. Besides, you might come across information in other questions that will give you clues about how to answer the difficult questions.

It is very important not to be superstitious when taking an objective test. Some people think that a pattern like TFTFTF on a true-false test means that the next answer must be T; or that a pattern like a,b,c,a,b,c on a multiple-choice test means that the next answer must be an a. There is no guarantee that the pattern will continue.

One of the most difficult things about objective tests is that sometimes several choices for answers look reasonable, but you can only choose one. The best approach is to first try and figure out the correct answer before you even look at the choices. Then, even if you see the answer you guessed, you should still look at the other choices to make sure that none seem more correct than your guess. If you do not know the answer at first, read each of the choices very carefully, and eliminate the ones that you know are wrong. In this way, you are more likely to arrive at the correct answer by a process of elimination.

Here are some more things that people are superstitious about when taking objective tests. Some people might tell you not to pick choices that use words like "all," "none," "always," "never," "must," and "only," because these words are too strong to apply to anything in life. They might tell you instead to pick choices with words that allow for some exception, like "sometimes," "frequently," "rarely," "often," "usually," "seldom," and "normally."

Some people are even superstitious about picking the first or last choice on an objective test, because they think the teacher feels more comfortable about putting the right answer in the middle; or that you should select the choice that is shorter or longer than the rest, because it is more likely to be true. One of the most common pieces of advice you get is never to change your first answer because it is usually correct.

Even if you think there may be some truth in this advice, you should avoid it because it is just superstition. The only real way to figure out what is true and what is false is to know the right answer, and that is up to you—not superstition!

I have some final advice for you about objective exams. If you have gone all of the way through an exam and you still do not know the answer to a question, then you might as well guess. Just think about it—you have a fifty-fifty chance of being right on a true-false test, and you even have a pretty good chance on a multiple choice test, depending upon the number of choices. Even on tests in which the teacher penalizes you (subtracts points) for being wrong, it still pays to guess if the penalty is small enough.

Problem Exams

Problem exams are the types of tests you take in mathematics and science classes. They test your ability to reason and solve problems. Some people are very nervous about mathematics; they have what is often known as "math anxiety." These people just freeze up at the idea of having to take a math test. Some people believe that a person is born with the ability to solve math problems, but natural ability is not always the most important thing. Even if you are not a natural mathematician, there are certain things you can do that will help you score higher on problem exams.

The type of questions that give students the most difficulty are word problems. As with essay exams, you should read through all of the word problems on an exam before you actually start to answer any one of them. As you read each question, you should underline key words that tell you what you are supposed to do. Also underline important information, such as amounts that are given, units of account, and so on. In the margin of your test paper, you should write down any formulas that you want to remember, or how you will go about solving the problem.

After you do this for the first problem, you should quickly move to the next question and do the same thing. After you finish reading all of the word problems in this way, you should have a good idea of the ones that will be easy and the ones that will be difficult. If the teacher gives you a choice, always pick the problems that are the easiest and figure out how much time you have to do each one. Always work on the easiest problems first and come back to the more difficult ones later on, for the same reasons that I mentioned when I talked about essay exams.

As you go back to work each problem in detail, make sure that you know exactly what you are supposed to do. It is a good idea to list all of the unknowns that are you are supposed to find, so you will not forget any of them. Sometimes it helps to list given information in a table, or even to draw a picture that describes how you plan to go about solving the problem. Another thing that helps is to predict a reasonable answer before you start to work, so you can compare it with the answer you actually get when you solve the problem.

Let's go through a simple example that illustrates how to use these principles to solve a math problem. Suppose you are asked to solve the following problem on a test:

Calculate the <u>area</u> of the following figure:

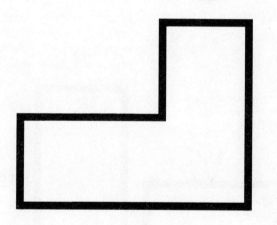

2 ft

4 ft

2 ft

5 ft

Notice that I have underlined key words that tell me what I am supposed to do, and important given information such as the length and width of the figure.

I could also have written down the formula, Area = Length × Width, or A = L × W, the formula for calculating the area of a rectangle—but the figure above is not really a rectangle. As I look more closely at the figure above, I realize that I can divide it up into two rectangles. The width of the first rectangle is 2 feet, and its length is 3 feet (5 feet minus 2 feet). The length of the second rectangle is 2 feet and its width is 4 feet.

Now I can apply my formula to calculate the area of each rectangle, and then add them together to get the area of the entire figure. I also notice that the area of the entire figure must be less than 20 square feet, which is the area of a rectangle that is 5 feet by 4 feet. Now draw the two rectangles, put in their dimensions, and calculate the answer:

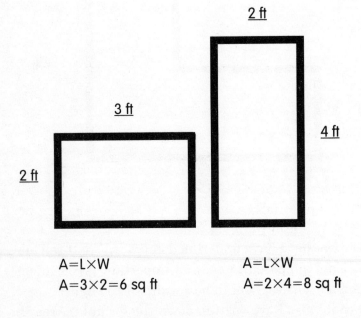

A=L×W
A=3×2=6 sq ft

A=L×W
A=2×4=8 sq ft

Area of the entire figure=6+8= ⟮14 sq ft⟯

I know you have heard this a thousand times from your teachers, but it is always important to *show all of your work*. Don't try to do very complicated calculations in your head. If you make a silly mistake and get the wrong answer, when you show your work the teacher can at least see where you went wrong and give you some credit. If you don't show your work, the teacher does not have any idea of what was going through your head.

In problem exams, it is important to be very careful in your work. If you are sloppy or in a hurry, it is very easy to make errors in your calculations. When you finish your work on each question, go back and read the question again to make sure that your answer includes everything you were supposed to do. Finally, draw a box around each of your answers so it will be easy for your teacher to find them. You don't want the teacher to overlook your answer because it is buried in a bunch of calculations.

Although these steps will improve your ability to solve problems, sometimes things may not go so smoothly. You may come across problems that are very difficult to solve. This is not unusual because many problem exams are designed to test your thinking ability.

If you come across a problem that is very difficult to solve, first think about other similar problems that the teacher presented in class, or ones you had for homework, and the methods that were used to solve them. Sometimes you can substitute one value for another, or use a different approach that will make the problem easier to figure out. Just remember that there are often many different ways to solve a particular problem.

Sometimes you can attack a problem from a different direction and figure it out. If a question is very long and hard, it may help to break it up into smaller parts that are easier to deal with. That's what we did in the problem above. Even if you forgot the formula for the area of a rectangle, you might still be able to get the correct answer if you understand the concept of area. "Area" is the same as the number of square boxes, measuring one unit in length by one unit in width. Applying this to the problem above:

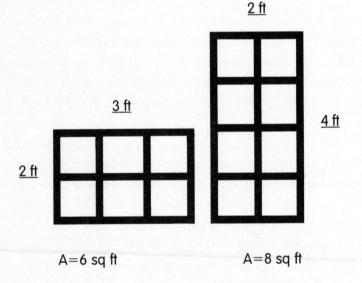

A=6 sq ft   A=8 sq ft

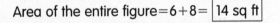

Area of the entire figure=6+8= 14 sq ft

What I always liked about problem exams is that I knew there was a correct answer. This gave me the energy to keep trying different things until I found it. Whatever you do, don't give up! If you get frustrated and give up, the teacher is not going to give you any credit. If you can only solve part of the problem, you should still write it down; at least you will get some credit. The additional credit you get may be the difference between an A and a B!

Open-Book Exams

Some teachers may give you an open-book exam, in which you take the test in class, but you are allowed to use materials such as notes, books, or "cheat sheets." Some teachers may say that you can use only certain materials, while others may say that you can use anything you want. The open-book exam measures not only your ability to understand information, but also your ability to locate, organize, and present it.

There is one important thing that all students need to know about open-book exams: Just because you can use a lot of extra materials to take the test, this does not mean that you do not have to study or prepare for it. You can have all of the materials available that you want, but if you don't know how to use them you are likely to run into trouble. In fact, you may have so many materials that you do not know what to do with them. It is still very important to read all of the assigned books, and learn how to use the charts, tables, and formulas in them, *before* you take the test.

If your teacher allows you to use a cheat sheet for an

open-book exam, you should do the work ahead of time to make sure it is carefully organized. Only include information that is important, not everything you reviewed for the test. It is impossible to write down everything on a single sheet of paper and, even if you could, you would not be able to find the information you need during a test.

Here are some tips that will help you put together an effective cheat sheet. Create an index that points to the locations of particular subjects or topics in your class notes or textbooks. Consider the question on the First Amendment that we answered earlier. If this was in an open-book test, you might have created an index that listed the page numbers in your class notes and textbooks that describe the First Amendment and discuss its importance. This would have enabled you to find the information quickly during the test.

Always be sure that you know exactly which materials you can use during an open-book exam. It would be very disturbing if you planned to use a certain book or notes for the test, and then found out later that these are not allowed. Also, don't be so overly confident that you neglect to use materials that the teacher allows, just because you think you know the subject by heart. These materials may help you do better on the test, so why put yourself at a disadvantage? Your classmates will probably use them!

Take-Home Exams

A take-home exam is just another type of open-book exam. The only difference is that you have more time to complete it in the comfort of your own home. On most take-home exams, the teacher gives the students several days or a week (or more) to finish the exam, and allows them to use any materials they want. Because of this, the teacher has to make the take-home exam more difficult than the in-class exam; otherwise, everyone would get an A.

I can remember that when I was a student I never liked take-home exams. I thought they were often very long and difficult. I would always rather take an in-class exam because my study methods gave me an advantage over the other students, and these exams were usually shorter and easier. Some teachers do not give take-home exams because they take much longer and are more work to grade. Nevertheless, you need to know how to take this type of exam in case you get one.

The biggest mistake that most students make on take-home exams is not starting soon enough; then they do not have enough time to complete the exam. Many students, knowing that they have a week to complete the exam, may not start working on it until a day or so before it is due. At this point they get very nervous and start to panic, and as a result do not do their best work.

Always try to start working on your take-home exam as soon as you can. A good approach is to divide the total time needed to complete the exam by the number of questions, and allow yourself this amount of time to answer each of the questions. Try to stick to this schedule, and avoid the temptation to put the test off until later.

Another trick with take-home exams is knowing where to look to find the answers. Because take-home exams are often complicated, you may have to look beyond your notes and textbooks. You may even have to search through outside readings, and this is another reason to get started early. These books are often a good place to look. Now that you know how to preview a book effectively, you can scan through it to see if it contains an answer. But don't get so excited about looking for answers in distant places that you forget to look for them in your notes and textbooks.

Here's some more good advice on take-home exams: answer only the question that is asked, not everything you can find to fill up space. You do not want to give your teacher the impression that you do not know the answer, and are trying to fake it. Try to put your answers in your own words rather than writing down sentences directly out of books. This will show that you have a good understanding of the material. It is also a good idea to type, rather than write, your answers. This will make it easier for your teacher to read your answer, and may even earn you some extra points. I will be giving you a lot more advice on writing in the next chapter, "How to Write a Paper."

Oral Exams and Reports

Teachers are more likely to ask students to make an oral report than to take an oral exam. When I was working on my Ph.D. dissertation, I had to take a very detailed oral exam in front of six professors to defend my research. They asked me very detailed questions that I had to answer in order to get my degree. Students who have done a research paper are often asked by the teacher to make a presentation to the class. Although this is not really an oral exam, the teacher will probably give you a grade that may be a significant part of your overall average. For this reason, it is important for you to know how to give an effective oral report.

Teachers ask students to give oral reports for a couple of different reasons. First of all, these reports give other students in the class an opportunity to learn about your research, and you in turn will learn about theirs. Second, giving oral reports helps to develop your speaking and presentation skills. As you continue with your education, and eventually with your occupation, you will find that there will be many occasions when you have to make presentations. You may even have to take a detailed oral exam like the one I had to take. The more experience you get, the better you will perform.

Now, I know that many students have an intense fear of getting up in front of the class and making a presentation. They are afraid that they will be the center of attention, and the worst thing imaginable might happen—when they open their mouth they won't know what to say. The main reason people are afraid of giving talks is that they do not give enough of them, so the whole experience feels unnatural. If you give talks frequently, and know the right way to do it, you will find that it is really no different than having a conversation with your friends. In fact, you may even start to enjoy them.

One of the most important things in giving an oral presentation is to pick a subject that you find interesting. Most teachers give students at least some choice in picking a subject. It will be a lot easier to conduct research on a subject that you find interesting, and you will be a lot more knowledgeable and enthusiastic when you make your presentation.

The biggest mistake that students make in giving presentations is to stand up in front of the class and read word for word from something they have written. If you think about it, this is really pretty boring, and you wouldn't want to hear someone else make a presentation that way. There is little or no eye contact with the audience, the words come out sounding very unnatural, and everyone gets the impression that you are either nervous or don't know what you are talking about.

The right way to approach a presentation is to prepare an outline of what you are going to say in advance. The outline might be very similar to the structure of your research report. The advantage of the outline is that it lets you see the order and content of what you are going to say, so you can make sure that it makes sense and nothing important is left out. When you prepare your outline, the trick is to write fairly short phrases that will remind you of what you are going to say, not long sentences that will tempt you to read them in their entirety. If you do it right, a few words or phrases will remind you of a lot of things to talk about.

Let me give you an example. Suppose you have to give a talk in speech or English class, and the teacher suggested that you pick a subject you are very interested in or knowledgeable about. (By the way, this is very good advice because you will always do a better job talking about a subject you like and know.) You have just finished building a tree house in your back yard, and want to share your experience with others. You put together an outline that looks something like the following:

Building a Tree House

I. Why I decided to build a tree house.
   A. A place to meet with my friends.
   B. Wanted to sleep outdoors.
   C. Like to build things.

II. Preparing to build the house.
   A. Find a good spot.
      1. Tree limbs need to be large and strong.
      2. Limbs must have right angle to support structure.
   B. Build a ladder up to work area.
   C. Measure out distances and draw the floor plan.
   D. Purchase materials.
      1. Metal support brackets.
      2. Nails and steel rods.
      3. Lumber.
         a. Plywood.
         b. Two-by-fours.
   E. Obtain the right tools.
   F. Line up people who will help.

III. Constructing the tree house.
   A. Build the foundation.
   B. Construct the frame.

        1. Build the walls and windows.

        2. Install a door.

    C. Install the roof and waterproofing.

    D. Furnish the tree house.

IV. Conclusion.

    A. Tips for other builders.

    B. Enjoying its use.

    C. Why others should build a tree house.

After finishing your outline, you will be able to make sure that you have covered everything and that it flows in the right order. (Your mother or father might remind you that you had to get approval from the neighborhood review board to create such a structure in your back yard.) All you have to do is follow the outline when giving the speech. Each entry in the outline reminds you what to talk about. You can fill in the details by giving examples or telling anecdotes.

The best way to get comfortable about the idea of giving a talk is to think everything through in advance. Think about how the teacher will introduce you, how long you will speak, whether you will use only your outline or other materials, and if the class will be asking you questions at the end. Play it through in your mind, almost like a movie, so it will not feel unnatural when you get up in front of the class.

After you think your talk through, it is a good idea to practice it in front of relatives or friends, or even in front of a mirror. This will help you get comfortable with your outline and other materials, and give you the confidence to feel that you can pull it off successfully.

When giving a talk to a group, it is important to have an effective delivery. First of all, you should be enthusiastic about your talk, because this will get other people interested. Think about the best way to communicate with your audience, and how to express things in a way that will get their attention. During your delivery look into their eyes, moving from person to person in the classroom, rather than staring off into space. Also, move your body rather than standing there like a statue. Vary the tone of your voice so your talk won't sound boring.

When I think about the interesting talks I have heard over my lifetime, they have been relevant, interesting, humorous, and short. You want to entertain people and teach them something new and interesting. They won't remember everything you say, so think about the main points you want to make. Think about how to present your information during the talk but, above all, think about the most important thing you want them to remember when the talk is over. For example, in the talk about "Building a Tree House," you might want to convince others that building a tree house is an interesting and fun thing to do.

When I was young, I disliked getting up in front of the class to make a presentation. As I have grown older, public speaking is one of things that I truly enjoy. I now realize that it provides the opportunity to meet new people, to learn some new and interesting things, and to practice my speech-making skills. I think that you will start to feel the same way, especially as you gain more experience.

What to Do During the Test—
Run the Good Race . . .

1. Write clearly on written exams, because this will increase your chances of doing well. Start out by writing your name and other information very clearly, and then organize your responses to the exam questions very carefully. The teacher will be more likely to understand your answers if you use good penmanship and practice the rules of good grammar, accurate spelling, sound paragraph construction, and solid theme development. Besides, your teacher will appreciate your good penmanship.

I always chose to write my answers to essay questions in pencil, if the teachers allowed it, because I could go back and erase parts I wanted to change. This produces a neater-looking essay than writing in ink and scratching out lines. In an objective exam, even though you are not writing sentences, you should mark your answers very carefully and clearly.

I can remember an exam I took when I was in college—my professor told me that he added five extra points to my score because I had written my answers so clearly. He also told me how hard it was to read the other students' papers because their writing looked like "chicken-scratch." Although most teachers or professors would not admit this to their students, I think something similar is going through their minds. They really appreciate it when you make their job a little easier and more pleasant.

Another reason not to do a sloppy job in writing your

answers on an exam is that you might give your teacher the impression that you do not know the complete answer, and are trying to fake it. Teachers are aware that some students are trying to cover up, so they do not give them a break just because their writing is unclear. In fact, even if you do know the complete answer, the teacher may not be able to understand it if your writing is very bad. So you end up hurting yourself anyway!

2. Go back and review your answers. Even if you finish your test ahead of time, and you thought it was easy, it is still a good idea to go back and review your answers during the time that is left. It is all too easy to make a careless mistake, especially if you have been writing rapidly.

You might have tried to be very careful in answering the questions, but there are any number of things that could have gone wrong. In an essay test, your responses may be filled with poor grammar, incorrect spelling, unclear writing, poor paragraph construction, and so forth. In an objective test, you may have marked your answer to a question on the wrong space on the answer sheet and several of your next responses will be out of order. In a problem test, you may have used the wrong formula or made incorrect calculations. You can usually catch and correct many of these types of errors by using the remaining time to review your answers very carefully.

Here are some tips that will help you in reviewing your answers. As you read your answer again in an essay test, ask yourself if you have really given a good response to the question. If other pieces of information come to your mind during the review, then add them to your answer at the appropriate point. I always found that I could come up with more to say if I reviewed my answers at a later time.

I have taken a lot of tests during my lifetime, and in almost every one some students turned their test papers in to the teacher before the time was up. They either thought they knew too little and could not finish the exam, or they were very confident and thought they knew it all. Some may have been trying to impress the teacher or other students with how much they knew. I can also remember hearing some of the same students complaining outside in the hallway, or before the next class, that they knew the right answer all the time but forgot to write it down on their test paper.

Don't fall into the same trap! It is just plain stupid not to use all of the time a teacher gives you to complete an exam. Any product made by man can be made better with more time and effort, and this includes exams. I was always the last person to leave the classroom during an exam, because I was reviewing my answers right up to the very end. Don't turn in your exam paper until your teacher tells you to leave the classroom.

My final advice to you about taking any type of exam is *never cheat*. I shouldn't even have to give you this advice because it is common sense, but I will anyway because I know there is a lot of cheating going on out there. Some students use "cheat sheets" during a closed-book exam, and others attempt to steal answers by reading them off of their classmates' papers.

Cheating is stupid for several reasons. First of all, you might get caught and the consequences could be very serious. The teacher will not think much of you as a student, and you may never be able to get back his or her respect. Even more serious, you might get an F on the test or the course, or even be suspended or expelled if your school has a tough policy on cheating. Second, you should not cheat because when you copy a classmate's work, you are assuming that someone else in the classroom knows a better answer to the question than you do. If you have been following my study system, you probably know more than anyone else in the class, so you need to trust yourself. The third and final reason for not cheating is a matter of personal pride. Even if you succeeded in cheating, you would not feel good about your grade because you did not earn it fairly!

This has been a long chapter on how to take various types of tests, but it is a very important one to your success. If you have understood everything I have discussed, then you are on the right road to becoming a "testwise" student—but more will be required! It is not enough to know everything I have presented; you need to *practice* it. And like any sport or activity, the more you practice, the better you will get.

RECAP

To become a testwise student you must:

1. be prepared before taking tests,

2. know how to take different types of tests,

3. use your time wisely,

4. review your answers to the questions.

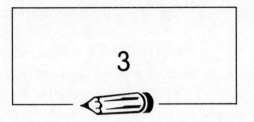

3

How to Write a Paper

(. . . and be proud of what you have written!)

Donna started playing the piano right around the time when she was learning how to walk and talk. It didn't sound like music back then, but she can still remember the joy of pounding on the keys and listening to the different notes. Playing the piano is something of a tradition in Donna's family. The question was not whether you were going to play the piano, but when you were going to start.

Through the years Donna attended piano class several times a week, and practiced at home whenever she had a chance. It was a lot of effort but it didn't seem like work, because playing the piano was something that Donna loved to do. She particularly liked the feeling of accomplishment that came from becoming a better mu-

sician, and the feeling of joy that her music brought to other people.

All of this was flashing through Donna's mind as she sat on the stage waiting to hear the results of the latest competition she had entered. She was the last person to play; her selection was a piano concerto by Mozart. She had played the piece without making any significant mistakes, which was more than could be said for most of the other contestants. First prize was really big—the opportunity to go on to regional and possibly national competition, which would help her chances of getting a college scholarship in music.

When the judges announced that Donna had taken first place, she was overcome, first by relief and then by joy. Donna's music teacher congratulated her on the victory, but then quickly added that the performance would need to be better at the next level of competition. Although Donna had not made any significant mistakes, she had read the music for the entire piece, which gave it a kind of mechanical sound. Donna's teacher wanted her to memorize the entire piece by heart for the big competition coming up in two months.

Two months was plenty of time to prepare, but Donna decided that she would start her preparation right away rather than wait. Her goal was to memorize a significant part of the concerto each week, so that by the end of the first month she would know the entire piece by heart. This would give her all of the second month to practice her performance and put more feeling into her music.

To make a long story short, Donna practiced as planned, and was able to take first place again at the next level of competition.

. . .

There is a significant moral to this story. Donna was successful with her musical performance not only because she knew what she was doing and worked hard, but also because she started to prepare well in advance. The same skills apply not only to music, but also to writing. You need to know how to write a good paper, and you must start early enough so you will have time to finish everything in an orderly manner.

The ability to write—and write well!—is a very important skill to have in a highly developed society such as ours. As a form of communication, writing is just as important in our society as speaking. You probably do some form of writing almost every day of your life, such as a letter written to a friend, a note written to a parent, or a report written for your teacher. Much of the communication in the business world is in a written form.

Writing is one of the most important forms of communication that you will have with your teachers in school. I am not just talking about communication in your English class—I am talking about communication in all of your classes. The grade you receive in a subject is largely the result of what you write on exams. In many courses other than English, you will have written assignments such as essays, reports, book reviews, and term papers. Next to reading, as a student you will probably spend more of your time writing than doing anything else.

Even though writing is a very important skill, many people in our society are not very good at it. I am not just talking about young students. Many adults do not write very well, and this has prevented some of them from getting better jobs. Writing is a problem for many people because they never learned the correct way to write when they were going through elementary, middle, and high school. In fact, some people have just given up. They feel that there is nothing they can do to improve their writing.

I have a confession to make to you. When I was a young student I did not like to write. My papers would come back from the teacher all marked up in red, and often with a low grade. Even when I was an older student in college I did not like to write, and sometimes I would not take a course if it required a term paper. My problem was that I had never learned the correct way to write, so the whole experience was very unpleasant. Now, this may seem like a strange confession to make, especially coming from an author who writes books. But I can also tell you that once I learned how to write, I really started to enjoy it. In fact, writing is now a leisure activity for me, just like going to the movies is a form of leisure for many other people.

Of all the writing assignments that students get in school, the one that gives them the most trouble—and that they dislike the most!—is the term paper. Many students do not like term papers because they take so much time and work to write. They would rather be using this time to study other subjects, prepare for exams, play sports, or just goof off. And even after you put in all of the time and work, there is no guarantee that you will get a good grade. Your "masterpiece" may come back from the teacher all marked up in red, with an instruction to do part of it over again. And you probably do not have a choice, because term papers often count for a third or more of your total grade.

Now, you may be wondering why your teacher puts you through all of the trouble of writing a term paper. You might even be thinking that it is a cruel form of punishment, like being forced to eat liver and onions (that would be a cruel form of punishment for me!). I can tell you right now that this is not why the teacher wants you to write a term paper, and that if you think this way you are already off to a bad start.

One obvious reason teachers assign term papers is because they want you to demonstrate that you have learned something about the subject you are studying. A less obvious reason is that they want you to develop skills you will need later in life, regardless of the occupation you decide to enter.

Another reason why some teachers assign term papers is to give students another chance to show what they know about a subject. As I said earlier, some bright students just do not do very well on an in-class test with fixed time limits. The term paper gives them a lot more time to think about a subject and present their findings in a written report.

Let's say that the teacher has just given you an assignment to write a term paper. How do you go about it?

To write a good term paper, you need to investigate a subject in detail. You have to show that you know how to use the correct methods to research a subject. This may require you to use the resources in a library to collect information about the subject. Then you have to organize the information that you have collected. Finally, you will need to present your findings in a well-written paper. These are the steps that an author such as myself goes through in writing a book, and they are also the steps that any researcher goes through in investigating a subject.

Pick a Good Subject

The first thing you need to do is to decide upon a good subject to write about. It takes a lot of time and effort to write an excellent paper, so you should definitely pick a subject that you find interesting.

You might choose a subject in which you have always been interested, or something your teacher suggested that caught your attention. If your teacher assigned subjects to students in the class, then you really do not have a choice. But I have found that most teachers give students some say in the subjects they choose for a paper.

One piece of advice is to pick a subject that is fairly narrow. If it is too broad you may not be able to deal with the subject matter in the time and space available to write the paper. If you are having difficulty picking a subject, it is okay to start off with something general, but then work quickly to narrow it down.

As an example, suppose you want to write about World War II. This is a very broad subject that would be difficult to write a term paper on. You might want to focus instead on the bombing of Pearl Harbor, which would be much more manageable. Sometimes it takes a while and some effort to narrow a subject down to something that can be addressed in a paper. Don't be reluctant to ask your teacher for advice if you are having difficulty narrowing down the subject.

Ask Specific Questions

Once you have decided on a subject, the next step is to develop specific questions that you want to answer in the paper. You should write these down. Your questions may be very broad at this point, and they may even change over time, but at least they will help you to organize your thoughts as you do your research. Without specific questions and issues, you won't know what you are looking for in your research.

To continue with our example, suppose you are writing on the bombing of Pearl Harbor during World War II. You might formulate the following questions:

1. When did the bombing occur?
2. Why did the Japanese decide to strike when they did?
3. What was the extent of the damage caused by the bombing in terms of men, ships, airplanes, and buildings?
4. What did the U.S. do to retaliate for the bombing?
5. How did the bombing affect the course of the war?

You might come up with more questions as your research progresses. If you are having difficulty formulating questions at the early stages of your research, your teacher may again be willing to provide some help. This will also tell you something about the questions the teacher thinks are important.

Do Your Research

Now that you have developed specific questions for your paper, you will need to do research to get information to answer them. This means that you will probably need to read some books or articles about the subject. Some teachers mention or list relevant books and articles when they are helping students decide on a subject. If you feel that you do not have enough materials to read, you may need to ask your teacher for some additional suggestions. Also, each book or article that you find may have references to other written materials on the subject.

Another place to find additional reading materials is in the library. Every student needs to become familiar and comfortable with the library. When I was a student writing papers, I used to look through the card catalog for books and articles I knew about, in order to find other reading materials on a subject.

Most libraries now have a much more efficient method for finding information, using computer searches. You just put in a few key words and these systems will give you a list of books and articles you can find on a subject, not only in your library, but in others as well. Many of the systems can give you a printout showing a list of books and articles with brief summaries so you will know what each book is about. Don't be shy about asking the librarian for help in using these systems.

As you review various books and articles, you can use the methods you learned in "How to Read a Book" to find out if these are relevant to your subject. By looking through the table of contents, headings, summaries, graphs, and so on, it should only take you a few minutes to figure out whether a book will be useful to you.

Once you have found a book that is relevant to your subject, then you should take very careful notes as you read it. You should copy down information that addresses the questions you are trying to answer—not everything you read. Rather than writing down the information word for word, try to put it into your own words. In this way, it will make more sense to you later on. If you see something that you want to quote, write it down with quotation marks around it and check it carefully to make sure it is accurate.

One of the best ways to find information is through the Internet. If you do not have a personal computer at home, you might be able to gain access to the Internet through a computer at school or in your local library. By typing a few key words, such as "Pearl Harbor," you can use any number of search engines to find a wide range of information about your subject.

Whether you are quoting someone or just writing down their thoughts, it is important to give them credit. Write down important information that you can use in your references or footnotes, such as the title of the book, the name of the author, the name of the publishing house, where and when it was published, and the page number, or the names of sites where you found information on the Internet. It is a good idea to keep track of all of the relevant information as you read, so you won't have to look it up later on. This would be a lot of work, and no fun!

Everyone seems to have their own system for keeping track of information and thoughts while they are doing their research. You can write down your thoughts on plain notebook paper or on three-by-five-inch index cards. It is better to write on only one side of the paper or cards so you can spread them out, see what you have, and move them around to organize your information in different ways. This would be very difficult to do if you had written on both sides of the paper. Some people even like to use a tape recorder to keep track of their thoughts. It really does not matter what you do. You should use what you are comfortable with, but use the same system throughout your research so you will know what information you have later on.

You will need to do a lot of reading to come up with new thoughts. The idea is not only to show that you have learned what other people have already said, but to come up with some thoughts of your own. This is what really excites teachers when they read a research paper. Now, I don't have to tell you that this is a very difficult thing to do. But you can increase your chances of coming up with something new if you use *creative thinking*.

I am sure that you have heard the word "creative" before. It is a word that we all would like to hear about ourselves. If you want to be a creative thinker, there are several things that you need to do.

First you must gain a clear understanding of the questions you are trying to answer. For example, we formulated some specific questions in the example above concerning the subject of Pearl Harbor. Think very carefully about the questions you are trying to answer, so you will know exactly what information you are looking for.

Next, you need to collect as much information as possible to help you answer the questions. You were doing this when you were reading various books and articles about your subject, or looking up information on the Internet. The more you read, the more knowledge you will get, and the better you will be able to answer the questions.

Once you've collected your information, you should leave the subject alone for a while and let your mind work on it. You might not consciously be thinking about the questions you are trying to answer, but your mind is probably still working on them. If this sounds strange to you, just think about all of the times when you have thought deeply about something, perhaps trying to remember someone's name. Sometimes the name will just pop right into your head a couple of hours or days later, even though you are not actively thinking about it. The same type of process goes on with creative thinking.

All you need to do in the last stage is to compare the various answers you came up with against your original questions, to see which ones are the best answers. Be sure to write down these answers in your notes.

As you have been doing your research, your questions may have changed. Your general questions may have become more specific. This is natural, because sometimes it is very hard to come up with specific questions before you start doing your research. As you learned more about a subject, you may have even gone in a different direction and asked new questions.

After you have finished doing your research, the next step is to organize it into something that makes sense.

Develop an Outline

Having an outline for writing a paper is just as important as having a blueprint for building a house. You wouldn't try to build a house unless you had some plan showing what goes where, and in what order. An outline for a paper shows you how to organize your thoughts, and the order in which to present them. Your outline is a plan that shows you how to write your paper.

As you did your research and took your notes, you probably noticed that the information could be put together in a way that makes sense. For example, the information might be organized according to when (the time) it happened, where (the location) it happened, or how (the order) it happened—what came first, second, and so on. You can see more clearly how to bring the information together if you put it into an outline.

One of the things we all have learned from our earliest years in school is how to put together an outline. The title of your outline should be the same as the title of your paper. Major subjects are indicated by Roman numerals (I, II, III . . .), and minor subjects within them are indicated by capital letters (A, B, C . . .), indented under the major subjects. You can then show other information under these minor subjects using Arabic numerals (1, 2, 3 . . .) and small letters (a, b, c . . .), all indented under the subjects they describe.

A good illustration of the structure of an outline is the one I provided earlier on the subject of "Building a Tree House." (See page 75.)

A good outline has short phrases that describe the main ideas, not long sentences and paragraphs that you would actually write in the paper. When you have put together an outline in this way, it will give you a complete look at how all of the information is arranged. The outline will help you to see the best way to organize your thoughts. You can see how the subjects relate to one another, and whether you have repeated or contradicted yourself. It will also help you see where in the paper to include new ideas.

Sometimes it takes a while to develop a good outline, but it is a very important step that will help you write a good paper.

After you have finished with your outline, the next step is to index all of the information from your readings to each part of the outline. In other words, you write the number or letter from each subject in the outline on the relevant pages of notes that you took when doing your readings. This will give you the ability to organize your information in such a way that you will know what goes where in the paper. You are now ready to write your first draft.

Write Your First Draft

For many people, the hardest part of writing a paper is getting started. The thought of writing a paper can be so unpleasant that they will find almost any excuse to avoid starting. The best way to get around this problem is to sit down at your desk, take out some blank paper, and *just start writing!*

The First Draft

The *beginning*, or introduction, is very important because this is where you tell readers what your paper is all about, and make them interested in reading further. It is also where you should raise any questions that you want to answer. Try to keep your introduction fairly short, because readers will be anxious to start reading the rest of your paper if you have succeeded in getting their interest.

The introduction can be difficult to write because you have not yet written the paper, and don't know everything that you will include. In fact, once you have completed your paper you will probably make changes to your introduction. Some writers do their introduction at the very end, after they know how their paper has turned out. I think, however, that it is good to write at least something for an introduction before you get started with the main body of the paper. This will help you to get warmed up for writing the paper.

To write the *middle*, or body of your paper, all you have to do is include your notes in the right places in your outline. The major subjects in your outline become the chapters or major headings in your paper. The notes you took from your readings fill out the paper in the right places under the headings. Make sure that your headings stand out by using bold print or indentation, as I have done in the chapters of this book.

I don't have the time or space to go over all of the rules of good writing in this book; after all, that is why you take courses in English all through school. But there are a few important rules that I want you to remember, which will make you a better writer.

The most important rules concern making good paragraphs. The first or second sentence of the paragraph, which is called the topic sentence, tells the main idea of the paragraph. Everything else in the paragraph should relate back to the topic sentence. The other sentences support the topic sentence through the use of facts, examples, statistics, and so on. After all, the reader will be looking for some evidence that what you say is true.

Another important set of rules concerns the way you develop your ideas. Make sure that you present your paragraphs in a way that will help the reader understand your story. Sometimes the order of things is very important. As one of my teachers used to say, "Putting on socks and then shoes is very different from putting on shoes and then socks." Remember that your reader must be able to follow your thoughts to understand your message. Include words that will help your reader move from one idea to the next very easily—these are known as transitions. Also, your paragraphs, and sentences within them, should not all be the same length, or your writing could become boring.

There is a lot more to good writing than what I have told you here, and you should be learning it and practicing it in the English courses you take all through school!

The *ending*, or conclusion, is where you summarize the major findings of your paper. The conclusion should refer back to the introduction and answer any important questions that you raised there. In the conclusion, you should not only summarize what you have discovered, but also tell what other important subjects should be investigated, perhaps in another paper. Always remember that your conclusion contains the final thought that you will leave with the reader. This is what they will walk away with after they have put your paper down and moved on to something new. Make sure that they will remember your main message!

Although you are working on the first draft of your paper, try to make it as close to your final version as possible. This will reduce the amount of future work. You need to be flexible when rereading your first draft, and make changes where they make sense, even if you have to go back and change your outline. Just be sure that you make these changes to your outline as you go, so everything will be in agreement.

After you finish writing the first draft of your paper, let it sit for a while. During the time it is sitting, you may come up with new ideas that will make your paper even better. Be sure to keep track of these ideas so you will not forget them. After the paper has sat awhile, and no new thoughts seem to be coming, you will be ready to put your paper into final form.

Put Your Paper into Final Form

At this point you might feel that you are writing another whole paper. You might even ask the question, "Do I really have to do it?" The answer is, "Yes, you do!"

Even though your first draft might have looked very good when you finished it, once you start your rewrite, the problems in the first draft will become obvious. Even experienced writers like myself find it difficult to write something in final form the first time. Writers often go back and change their work again and again until they are satisfied with it.

Although some writers do not like to rewrite their work, it is a very important step that can make the difference between a good paper and an average paper. I like to compare it to the way an artist paints a picture. The artist puts a first coat of paint on the canvas to describe basic shapes, such as mountains and rivers. We can recognize the shapes at this point, but we also know that the painting is far from finished. With the next coat of paint, the artist begins to fill in the details so the basic shapes start to come to life and we can recognize them better. The artist continues to apply paint until he or she is satisfied with the painting.

I think that good writers do something very similar to good artists. They go over and over their writing until they are satisfied with the final result. In the process, they may have to remove words, sentences, or even paragraphs; change their words so they will be clearer; improve the order in which ideas are presented; develop a new introduction or conclusion; and so forth. Good writers use their erasers to make changes almost as much as they use their pencils to write things down. If necessary, you should be willing to rewrite your paper over and over again, until *you* are satisfied with it.

There is some other important advice you should follow when putting your paper into final form. *Use the style that your teacher has asked you to use!* If your teacher has asked you to type your paper on standard size paper and leave a one-inch margin all the way around, then do it. If the teacher has asked you to put footnotes at the bottom of each page instead of at the end of the paper, then do it. If the teacher has asked you to make references in a certain way, then do it. Be sure to follow all of the teacher's requests, because he or she will be looking for these when grading your paper. It is worth the extra effort!

Start Your Paper Early

I am going to end this chapter with the same advice that I gave you at the beginning. By now, you should realize that you need to begin working on your paper as soon as possible to finish all of the steps I have described. I can't tell you how much time you should be spending on each of the steps, but I can give you some general advice. You should spend about half of your time picking a good subject, asking specific questions, and doing your research. Use the second half of your time to develop an outline, write your first draft, and put your paper into final form.

If you don't start working on the first step of your paper soon after the teacher assigns it, then you will not have enough time to finish all of the other steps. You will need all of the time you can get to think creatively, come up with some new ideas, write your first draft, and put your paper into final form.

Many students tend to put off working on a term paper until the last minute possible. This gets in the way of other things they need to do, such as studying for tests—and writing a term paper under these conditions can be very unpleasant. I was guilty of this myself until I learned the correct way to write a term paper. As I said earlier, the main thing is to sit down at your desk, take out some blank paper, and just start writing!

In fact, if you start writing your term paper early enough, I think you will find the whole experience to be very interesting and enjoyable. It is very satisfying to learn more about a subject, come up with some new ideas, and see them written in your own words. When I finish writing a book, I really enjoy reading what I have produced, and seeing the whole thing in print with a fancy cover.

It takes a lot of time and effort to write an excellent paper, but it is a good investment that will bring you benefits later on. Who knows—you might even end up writing books like me! Remember:

RECAP

To write an excellent term paper:

1. pick a good subject you are interested in,

2. ask specific questions,

3. conduct your research,

4. develop an outline,

5. write your first draft,

6. put your paper into final form.

Start early!

WHAT YOU HAVE LEARNED

1. The Skills You Need to Learn

(. . . to become a straight-A student!)

RULE 1

To become an active reader, you should preview a book before actually reading it, and continually ask the kinds of questions that will help you understand the author's message.

RULE 2

To become a testwise student, you must know the methods for taking various types of tests and practice them on every test.

RULE 3

To write an excellent term paper, pick a good subject, ask specific questions, do your research, develop an outline, write your first draft, and then put your paper into final form. Start early!

2

How to Make Straight A's

(. . . and have fun doing it!)

WHAT YOU WILL LEARN

In this section I will show you the system that I developed for making straight A's in school. Although I developed this system while I was in graduate school, I have made changes so it will work for students at your grade level. When you read about the ten steps in my study system you may feel that you have heard some of them before. What is different in what I am showing you is how these methods come together to make a complete system of study.

Everything in my system works toward helping you understand the most of what your teacher says in class, and what you cover in your assignments. I start off by helping you to decide what types of subjects you will want to study. Then I tell you about the two subjects—English and mathematics—that I feel are most important to your success in just about everything you will study in school.

Working closely with your teacher, in the same way that you work closely with a coach in sports, is one of the most important things you can do. Your teacher is the one who gives you assignments, grades your tests and papers, and determines how fast and how far you will progress. I have found that most teachers test students on things that they cover in class, so it is important for you to understand everything the teacher says.

I think you will see that my study methods put you in the best position to learn the most from your teacher. Some of them are simple things like not missing class, and sitting in the front row so you will not miss what the teacher says in class. Others require more work on your part, such as doing homework and reading assignments before class, so you will understand more of what the teacher says in class.

As you go farther in school and the subjects become more difficult, it is important to take notes so you will not forget things. I will show you the best way to take notes in class, and how to review and add to them after class so you will be sure to understand your teachers' lessons. By doing this, you will find that you have already started studying for tests ahead of time, and when you actually sit down to study for a test it will be that much easier.

When I talk about studying for tests, I will show you how to figure out the types of questions your teacher is likely to ask. This will help you prepare well in advance, so the test will seem easier and you can score higher. I think you will see that taking tests is really no different than playing a game in one of your favorite sports; taking tests in school can be just as much fun, too.

The whole idea of my study system is to show you what and how much you need to study to become a straight-A student. Once you have done your work, you can put away your notes and books and not worry about whether you have studied enough. You will be confident ahead of time that you will make an A, and the only question will be, "How high will it be?" When you reach this point, that's when school will be more fun than you ever dreamed possible!

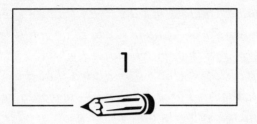

Take the Right Subjects

(. . . and school will be a lot easier!)

Ryan remembers when he first picked up a paper air-plane at three years of age. It seemed almost magical the way the light plane sailed through the air before coming to rest on the rug. Through the years his interest in air-planes grew as he put together various models of planes he got from his local hobby store. Soon he started putting engines on some of the models he built and flying the planes at the baseball field behind his house. He took out all of the books on flying he could find in the library and read them into the late hours. Ryan's greatest thrill came when his Uncle Jim, who is a commercial airline pilot, gave him a tour of the cockpit in a jumbo jet and took him for a ride.

Although Ryan was only eight years old when he took his first airplane ride, he knew right away that he wanted to be a pilot. Uncle Jim told Ryan that he should try to go to the Air Force Academy, where he could learn to fly jet fighters, and then maybe later fly jumbo jets with one of the big airlines. Uncle Jim added that it was not easy to get into the Air Force Academy—he would need to take some difficult subjects and make good grades to get in. Being a good athlete wouldn't hurt either.

Now that Ryan knew what he wanted, school took on a new meaning for him. Ryan started to think about school as if it was his job, and one that he needed to do well to move on to his next job as a pilot. He thought about all of the math and science courses that he needed to take, and the best order in which to take them. He also realized that it was important to do well in them, not only to get into the Air Force Academy, but also because they would make him a better pilot later on.

Everyone was amazed that Ryan worked so hard and was so serious about his studies. In fact, he always seemed to relate each new thing he learned in science and math to flying. And each time the teacher handed back a paper or test with high marks, Ryan felt that he was one step closer along the road to getting his wings to fly. When playing sports, too, Ryan always worked very hard, because he knew they would put him in better shape for all of the physical tests he would have to take at the Air Force Academy. Now every night when he goes to bed, Ryan dreams about what it will be like to be at the Academy, and how exciting it will be to become a pilot.

Ryan is a perfect example of a young man with a mission. He has a goal and knows exactly what he wants, and he also knows how to go about achieving it. Ryan's goal is what gives him energy and makes him work so hard in school. It is always easier to work harder at something when we think it has meaning and purpose, rather than something we have to do because we are told to do it.

Ryan is very lucky because he knew at an early age what he wanted to do with the rest of his life. Most people are not so lucky. Many do not know what they want to do when they enter college, and end up changing their major field of study several times while they are in college. Many people end up changing their careers several times during their lifetimes because they do not like what they are doing at work.

Because it can take a lot of time to decide on a career, I would advise you to take courses in school that give you the most possible choices later on. Most schools offer different groups of courses in programs with names like the "academic program," "the technical program," and the "general program." The academic program usually has the more advanced and difficult courses, and helps prepare students for college and a professional career. The technical program has a lot of useful courses that teach people how to work with machinery, which is good if you want to be doing this later on. The general program has the basic courses that you will need to graduate from high school and get along in our society, but does not include some of the more difficult courses in mathematics, science, and foreign languages.

I would recommend that you start off in the academic program, and stay in it as long as you can. The academic program may be more difficult than the other programs, but it will lead to the better jobs when you get out of school. Even if you decide that you want to switch to the technical or general program later on, it will be easy to do. It is much more difficult to switch from the technical or general program to the academic program, because you will not have had the basic courses you need.

The best approach is to talk to the guidance counselor at your school, along with your parents, to find out about the courses you will be taking in the academic program. Find out about the courses you will be taking for the rest of the school year, and also what courses you will be taking in future years. Try to get information on where the program is heading, and how much credit you will have when you get out of school. Sometimes you can even take advanced courses in high school that will count for credit in college.

Once you have decided on a program, it is very important to take courses in the right order. Many of the more advanced courses assume that you already know the information from an earlier course. For example, it would be very hard to take Algebra II if you have not already had Algebra I. It is similar to walking up stairs. If you go one step at a time you will not have any difficulty. If you try to go two or three steps at a time, not only will it be difficult, you may trip and fall. Never take courses out of the right order because you are interested in them or feel you can handle them.

If you are taking courses in the right order, and you are still having difficulty, you may need to take a closer look at your abilities as a student. Perhaps you did not learn as much as you should have from an earlier course in a subject, and that is why you are having difficulty

with the present subject. Or perhaps you have trans-
ferred from another school or state that was not as advanced in its course work, and suddenly you feel yourself
falling behind.

Fortunately there are things you can do to improve
your basic skills. Reading this book should certainly help
your study skills. But you may need additional help in
areas such as reading, writing, and comprehension (understanding what you have read). Here again, your
school guidance counselor can be very helpful. He or she
may be able to give you a test to find out which of your
skills need improvement. Some schools even have reading and study skills laboratories, with materials that
will help you read faster, understand more, and improve
your writing. If your problems are serious enough, you
may even need to take a special course to improve in
these skills. This could be a wise thing to do, the earlier
the better.

As you think about what courses to take in school,
remember that there are two subjects that are especially
important to your success—English and mathematics. I
would even say that if you are good in English and math,
then every other subject will be easy. Mastering these
two subjects is one of the first steps to becoming a
straight-A student. It should not surprise you that every
school requires students to take a certain amount of English and math to graduate.

Think about English for a minute. English is the language that we use to think, speak, read, and write. In
every subject, whether it is history, geography, music,
mathematics, or even English itself, you must know English to read books, do assignments, and take tests. You

may know a lot about a subject, but if you do not have a good understanding of the English language, you will not be able to show your teacher what you know. Students who do not understand English will have trouble not only with their courses, but also for the rest of their lives in everything they do.

Now think about mathematics. Although mathematics is interesting as a subject, we also study it because it is useful for so many other things. We live in a physical world in which numbers are very important. It is important not only to understand basic operations on numbers, such as addition, subtraction, multiplication, and division, but also mathematical relationships such as algebra, geometry, trigonometry, and so forth. When you are studying science, you need a knowledge of mathematics to understand the behavior of the physical world. If you think about it, the hardest part of most science classes is understanding the math. Math is a subject that you need to understand not only for your school subjects, but also for the rest of your life.

You should take as many courses in English and math as you can, even if you find them to be difficult. I think you will also find that the more courses you take in these subjects, the easier they become—and the easier every other subject becomes, too!

Another subject that is very important for you to take in today's world is computer science. You will find that you will be using computers in practically any occupation you enter when you get out of school. In fact, you will probably need to know how to use them just to be considered for many future jobs. That is why so many more courses on the subject are being offered in school. Computers are also going to be used more and more in the classroom as a way to educate students. You should take as many computer classes as you can, whether they involve learning how computers work, how to write computer programs, how to use the Internet, or even how to type properly.

Every program gives students the opportunity to take elective courses—which means that students get some choice in the types of courses they take. For electives, I would advise you to take courses that you find interesting. For example, you might be interested in art, music, or drama. I also think it is good for students to take courses in physical education all the way through school, even though some schools do not require it above a particular grade level. Physical education is fun, and gives your body a workout, which will help your mind work more clearly in your other classes.

You should think of school as your job, and your program of courses as what you do every day at your job. I would advise you to take school very seriously and stick with the program you are in, even if you are having some difficulty. Sometimes if you stay with a subject long enough, something clicks and you start understanding what it is all about. If, after a long enough period, you are just not catching on, then you might want to talk to your guidance counselor about making a change.

The way things work in our education system, once you finish certain courses, you move on to the next level. Keep your eye focused on what you are trying to accomplish, and be sure that all of these courses are leading up to something that you will someday do for a job. If you do this, school will be a lot more fun—and easier, too!

RECAP

If you want to become a straight-A student, then take subjects in the right order, and take the right subjects:

1. English,

2. math,

3. computer science.

Work with Your Teacher

(. . . because your teacher is your coach!)

Maria had her first introduction to art through finger paints. She can still remember the cool feeling of paint on her fingertips, and the way the brightly colored paints spread across the slippery paper into an interesting design. Through the years she used drawing pencils to sketch just about everything she saw inside and outside of her house. Then she moved up to watercolors and oil paints. She used the paint-by-number oil paints only for a short time because the colors didn't blend together, and she felt that she could draw more interesting pictures anyway.

When Maria got home from school each day, the first thing she did was draw and paint because it brought her so much satisfaction. Maria became very excited when she was filling out her schedule of classes for the next school year and realized she would be able to take art for an elective. This would give her even more time to draw and paint during the day. To help prepare herself, Maria got some books from the library on art techniques and studied them over the summer. Although Maria worked very hard on her oil painting over the summer, she still could not get things to come out the way she wanted them.

When Maria reported to school in the fall, the first things that caught her attention in the art classroom were the beautiful oil paintings that her teacher had painted. They looked almost as good as the paintings she had seen in the art museum, and they had a certain style that she particularly liked. She thought to herself, "If only I could paint like that!"

Through the school year, Maria's art teacher taught her almost everything she knew about art. She showed her how to prepare the canvas, when and how to use certain brushes, how to select and mix paints, and finally, how to get certain effects from the way you put paint on the canvas. It was almost like magic; Maria could not wait until the next class, when she would learn something new and be able to try it out on the canvas.

Maria and her teacher developed a special relationship over the years, even long after Maria had finished the art class. The teacher was happy to have a student who was so interested in the subject she loved, worked so hard in the classroom, and made so much progress. Maria was happy to have found a friend who also loved art, and who taught her so much.

Of course, Maria got an A in her art class. Every teacher is looking for students who are serious about the subject they are teaching, work so hard in the classroom, and show so much progress and ability. That's what education is all about! But the most important thing is not that Maria got the A. The most important thing is that she learned a lot, developed her ability, and found a valuable *friend*.

That's right—I said "friend." Your teacher is a friend in learning, and is there to help you increase your knowledge in a subject that is important, and probably will become even more important to you later on. Too many students think of their teacher as the enemy, someone who forces them to sit still in a chair and listen to something they are not interested in, and then punishes them by giving assignments and tests that are boring and difficult. Guess what—Maria never had this feeling about her art teacher because she was teaching Maria something that she wanted to learn.

One of the things that I do in my spare time is coach baseball. I work my players pretty hard, but they are always anxious to get out on the field and practice or play a game. Why? Because they love the game, that's why! I spend a lot of time teaching my players the mechanics of how to pitch, hit, and field the baseball. I show them video tapes, and then we go out on the field and they practice what they have learned. Even though this is a lot of hard work, they love it because they know it will make them better baseball players. The reward comes when they put it all together in a game, see themselves improve, and know they can move to the next level.

If you think about it, what a coach does on the athletic field is really no different from what a teacher does in the classroom. The first thing you need to do to work better with your teachers is to get interested in their subjects. Now, you may say that you're just not interested in English, math, history, or science, and you don't see how these subjects are going to help you anyway. I used to have these feelings myself. But, as you get older, you will realize that every subject you take in school is important, and most of them will help you later on in life. You will also realize that you might not have the same opportunity to learn about these subjects in the future.

I want you to think for a few minutes about your teacher. Teachers are people with a lot of education who could work at many different jobs, but they choose to teach because this is what they love to do. They love their subject, and they get a special feeling from working with their students and helping them to understand a subject that they feel is important.

Students need to realize that their teachers are working even harder than they are. Teachers had to go to college for many years, taking courses in education and other subjects so they could become teachers. Teachers spend hours after class reading about their subjects, preparing their class lectures, grading students' papers and tests, and so on. With all of their education, most teachers could probably get easier jobs that pay more money, but they teach because they love their job!

Teachers believe there is a best way to understand and teach a subject. Just think about it for a minute. Teachers have spent years and years studying a subject, and they know what helped them to understand it.

When teachers make a presentation in class, they are trying to show students the best way to understand a subject. If you can show your teacher that you have learned in one year what it has taken them a lifetime to learn, then that will get you an A every time!

Now that you understand where your teachers are coming from, let's talk about what you can do to work better with them. The first rule is that you should always show respect for your teachers, and let them know that you think their subject is important. You can do this by being interested in the subject, working hard, doing assignments on time, and not speaking out of turn in class. One good way to show your interest is to raise your hand when the teacher asks for a volunteer to do something. Most of all, do not cause any trouble or make noise in the class because this will create a bad impression. Once you create a bad impression, it will takes a lot of time and effort to make the teacher think more highly of you.

The next thing you should do is get to know your teacher as a person. We often think of teachers in their special role, but they are people just like your mom and dad or aunt and uncle. Spend some time talking to your teachers to get to know them better and find out what they are interested in. Talk to them about yourself so they will get to know you better. You may even find out that you have some similar interests.

One of the most important things you can do is to learn about your teacher's style in the classroom. Different teachers have different likes and dislikes, and you need to spend some time finding out about them. For example, if it really upsets the teacher when students are late, then do your best not to be late. If the teacher does not like to be interrupted by questions during his or her presentation, then wait until the teacher has finished the presentation before you comment or ask questions. If your teacher gets really upset by late assignments, then make an extra effort to be on time.

You should do all of these things because your teachers play a special role in your education. They are the ones who give you knowledge, make assignments, put together tests, and give you a grade. They determine whether you will get special awards and be assigned to the more interesting classes later on. How much you learn and how far you progress will be determined by how well you work with your teachers.

RECAP

To work well with your teachers:

1. **get interested in their subject,**

2. **learn their style in the classroom,**

3. **know about their likes and dislikes,**

4. **think of them as coaches in the classroom.**

3

Never Miss a Class

(. . . it will always catch up with you.)

Robert is a champion swimmer. He has always been comfortable in the water, right from the earliest years when his mother first held him in her arms and floated him in a pool. People who see Robert swim remark that he looks like a dolphin, the way he glides through the water so naturally without showing much effort. In fact, Robert feels more comfortable in the water, even during a big swim meet, than anywhere else in the world.

Robert did not become a champion swimmer overnight. It took a lot of hard work and dedication for him to reach this level. He joined the swim team at his local pool as soon as they would accept him, and he belongs to the swim team in an indoor pool during the colder months. Swimming requires a lot of effort and energy, and Robert had to attend practice every day. To make matters even more difficult, swimming practice started at six in the morning, so he had to get up at five every morning to finish up in time to get ready for school.

If you ask Robert about his secret for success, he will tell you that he never misses a swimming practice. There are times when he has stayed up late to finish a school assignment, or when he doesn't feel well, but even without much sleep he still manages to get up early to make swimming practice. Imagine jumping into a cold pool of water at six in the morning during the winter months when you are weak and tired. It doesn't bother Robert because he loves his sport, and this is where he wants to be.

Robert will tell you that never missing a swimming practice has made him better in two ways. First of all, he gets a good workout every day and naturally becomes stronger from all of the physical exercise. But second, and maybe more important, Robert has never missed any of the valuable instruction provided by his coach.

Robert competes in three different events: the freestyle, the backstroke, and the butterfly. Swimming is actually a very complicated and technical sport, and different methods and techniques will make you better in each event. By never missing a swimming practice, Robert has not only learned all of these techniques, he has had an opportunity to practice them in the pool. This has helped him to become a champion, because the winner in a swim meet may be only a fraction of a second ahead of the next person.

There is something else that I need to tell you about Robert, even though it does not relate directly to his swimming. Robert is a straight-A student at school who rarely, if ever, misses a day. You may say that it is easier for him to get to school because he has been up already for a couple of hours at swimming practice. But mainly, Robert has learned that the behavior that works in the pool also works in the classroom. By not missing any classes, he is there to hear everything his teachers say, and can practice it in his lessons. This is what makes him not just a champion swimmer, but also a champion student.

When I say never miss a class, I mean *never!* This is very important because most of the test questions will come from what your teacher presents in class. Every day in class, your teachers cover the subjects that they think are important for you to understand in their courses. They bring all of their knowledge into the classroom and present the ideas in ways that will be the easiest for you to understand.

Don't think for a second that your teacher is trying to trap or trick you. Teachers are more interested in what you know than in what you don't know. If you can show them that you understand everything they have presented in class, you are well on your way to getting an A in the subject.

You are taking a big risk when you miss class. First of all, the teacher may think that either you're not interested or don't care about the subject. Second, the test might include questions on subjects that your teacher covered when you were not there. If you are taking a test with three or four essay questions, and you skip one of the questions because you were not in class, then you may end up with a B or a C even if you know the answers to the other questions. Can you afford to take that chance?

When I say never miss a class, I also mean *never miss even part of a class.* You should always get to class on time and never leave early, because otherwise you might miss part of the teacher's discussion. The part you miss may show up later on a test. Teachers often use the first five minutes to review something from the last class, or to make an important announcement. They often use the last five minutes to summarize what was important in the class, or to make an assignment for the next class. Therefore, a lot of the important action occurs around the beginning and end of the class, and you should be there to hear it.

It is also important not to start packing up your school books and materials five minutes before class is over so you can beat your classmates out the door. This can create a disturbance while the teacher is trying to cover something important. Always practice good manners in the classroom, because this will affect the teacher's impression of you as a student.

If you want to create a good impression, get to class on time, be serious and interested in the subject, work very hard, don't make any noise, and leave the class in a polite manner. A good impression can make the difference between getting, say, an A or a B. As I said earlier, it is very hard to change a bad impression to a good impression.

Some students think that they can miss class and make up for it by going over the reading assignments more carefully. This can be a big mistake, because many teachers use more than the information from the readings to put together their class presentations. Teachers often use information that they learned as a student, making it more current to account for things that have happened since they went to school. If the school has bought new books for a course, the teacher might include some of this information in their class presentation, but not change the presentation completely. The safest thing you can do is attend every class so you will know exactly what the teacher presented. Don't try to second-guess the teacher!

Even if your teachers used only the reading assignments to put together their class presentations, you would still miss something significant by not going to class. Attending class changes you in an important way. When you go to class, your teacher introduces you to new ideas. You may leave the classroom with a different view of the world than the one you entered with.

You will continue to learn after you have left the classroom, even if you are not studying. Your mind will probably be reviewing the various things you learned during the day, even though you are involved in something else. Our minds are busy at work while we are doing everyday activities like getting dressed, eating, walking to class, or even talking to friends. You may find your mind silently going over facts you learned or problems you worked on that day, trying to make sense out of them.

There is an old Greek saying; "You can't step twice into the same river." Once the water has moved downstream, the river has changed. It is very similar with classes at school. Once you miss a class, it is gone forever.

The worst possible time to miss a class is near the end of the grading period. Unfortunately, this is the time when most students miss class. Their schedules are very busy, and they are trying to study for all of the tests coming up. It is important to attend these classes, because some teachers use them to review subjects covered earlier, or to let students know what will be tested on the final exam. Believe it or not, some teachers even go so far as to tell students the specific questions that will be on the final exam, or at least some possible questions.

Some teachers use the last class as a general question-and-answer period, in which students can ask about anything covered during the year, or anything they are wondering about. Some of these questions may even turn up on the final exam, so it is important to know their answers. If you miss these classes, your classmates who attended will have a big advantage over you on the test, and you might get a much lower grade.

If there is no way that you can attend class, then you should try to borrow the notes for that day from your teacher or one of your classmates. I think it is always better if you borrow your teachers' notes, because they will include just about everything that was covered in class. Some teachers, however, are not willing to lend students their notes, so you may have to get them from one of the better students in class who writes clearly.

Once you have the notes, you should rewrite them into your own notebook. If you do not understand everything that your teacher or another student has written, then you should ask them to explain it to you. This will help you keep up if you miss a class—but you should not make a habit out of being absent.

In the beginning of this book, I presented the report card for my son, Chris. Chris's example in attending class is a good one to follow. One of the things that helped him get straight A's for the entire seventh and eighth grades was that he missed only one class each year. On one occasion he had to stay home under doctor's orders, and on the other he came to work with me for "Bring Your Child to Work" day. If you're going to miss class, it should be for a very good reason.

If you wake up tired and sleepy, or just don't feel like going to class, don't be lazy and tell your parents that you want to stay home that day. One of my teachers used to say that there is only one excuse for missing a class: a death in the family—your own! You will be surprised at what you can do if you feel that you really have to do it.

RECAP

Never miss a class or be tardy because:

1. it creates a bad impression,

2. you will miss important information,

3. most test questions come from class lectures.

4

Always Sit Up Front

(. . . because that's where the action is!)

Samantha is a very good softball player. She made the varsity softball team at her school in the ninth grade, which is not an easy thing to do. Samantha's great strength is that she does a good job in practically any position on the field, including pitcher, catcher, infield, and outfield. The coach told her that he feels comfortable playing her anywhere on the field, and one day she will be one of the big stars on the team.

Samantha, or Sam as her teammates call her, hopes that "one day" comes real soon, because in the meantime she is on the second team. She is there for all of the practices and scrimmages, but in most games she is sitting on the bench. Her coach and other teammates tell Sam that it's not that she isn't a good player; it's just that younger players have to put in some time and pay their dues before moving up to the first team.

Sam accepts her situation with a good attitude, and in all of the games you will find her sitting right in the middle of the row in the dugout. It is almost as if Sam is actually playing in the game, because you can see her jumping up and down and waving her arms with each play, and you can hear her voice above everyone else's. The coach says that Sam's enthusiasm fires up all of the players on the team, and helps them to play better. He calls Sam the "tenth player on the field."

In the third game of the season, one of the players on the other team hit a line drive between second base and shortstop. Sam's best friend, Nikki, who was playing shortstop, dove toward the ball but was unable to get it. She got up with a limp and a look of terrible pain on her face, and waved her hand to come out of the game. The coach turned toward the dugout and faced all of the other players on the team, his eyes stopping on Sam right in the middle. "Sam," he said, "you're now the ninth player on the team. Go in there and play the game with as much energy as you have shown in the dugout."

Sam went in and finished up the game, and made several excellent plays that helped her team win because the score was so close. It turned out that Sam's friend, Nikki, had broken her ankle, and had to sit out during the entire season. Sam did such an excellent job in that one game that the coach made her a starter for the rest of the season. Sam felt terrible for her good friend Nikki, but she was glad that the coach gave her a chance to show what she could do.

. . .

Sam is convinced that the coach gave her a chance because she was always sitting there in the dugout, almost as if she was actually in the game. The coach could tell that Sam really wanted to play, and he got to know her better because they would often discuss different situations in games. Sam started sitting in the front row in all her classes at school, and found that the same type of thing started to happen. She became more interested in what was going on in the classroom, her teachers got to know her better, and her grades went up, too!

Baseball and softball players do not have a problem with sitting in the front row in the dugout during a game. In fact, there is only one row—the front row—in a dugout, and everyone wants to sit there so they can see what is going on. On the other hand, most students do not want to sit in the front row in their classes at school. They will do almost anything to avoid it. I have given many talks to students, and I always find that most people want to sit in the middle or back of the room rather than up front. Do you know why?

Most students would rather sit in the middle or back of the classroom because they feel threatened in the front row. They know that they will have less privacy in the front row, and the teacher is actually more likely to call on them to answer a question if they are up front. No one wants to look stupid by not being able to answer questions. You have to stay alert to sit in the front row, and that is exactly why you should sit there! You will get much more out of your teachers' presentations.

When you sit in the front row, you will be able to focus much better on your teacher and the blackboard. You will also be able to hear the lesson better. In addition, you are less likely to be disturbed by other students if they are moving around or talking with one another. In fact, when you are up front your teacher is more likely to recognize you as a good student, and will know that you are there to learn.

We can use our brains more effectively if we are in a good environment. The best place to use more of our brains is in the front row, because this is where we will not only learn more, but also remember more.

Most classes have twenty-five to thirty-five students, so not everyone can sit in the front row. If your teacher asks students where they want to sit, then volunteer to sit up front. If you still do not get a front row seat, then ask your teacher politely if you can move up front so you can hear better. Try to sit as close to the front as possible so you will get most of the benefits.

I will tell you right now that getting students to sit up front is one of the most difficult things to do. It is one of the easiest and most important steps students can take to improve their grades in school, and yet they still do not want to do it. Don't think that you can follow all of my other steps except this one, and still be a top student.

There is an old saying: "Time flies when you are having fun." People usually make the statement when they are talking about someone who is suffering. But the statement is really true. I always sat in the front row when I was in graduate school. I can remember going into classes and being so interested in my teachers' presentations that, when the class was over, I felt as if I had just walked into the classroom. I was listening so carefully to what my teachers were saying that I completely lost track of time. When you start doing this, the whole learning experience becomes more interesting and fun.

RECAP

Always sit up front because:

1. you can hear the lesson better,

2. you will not be distracted by others,

3. you have to be prepared to answer questions,

4. the teacher will know you are there to learn.

5

Complete Your Homework
Before Class

(. . . so you will be prepared in class!)

Billy started playing tennis when he was only four years old. He had to use two hands to pick up the tennis racket, which is probably one reason that he has a two-handed backhand today. They say it normally takes five years to develop a tennis game, but Billy was playing like a little professional by the time he was seven. He is a complete player who has mastered all of the shots. He has a beautiful serve and volley at the net, and can handle himself very well in the backcourt on either the forehand or backhand side.

By the time Billy was nine he had entered competition in his local area and was tearing up everyone in his age bracket. It was almost as if he did not have a single weakness, and couldn't be beaten. His tennis coaches realized that they had a rising young star, so they tried to make him even better by setting up matches with older players. Billy rose to the occasion, and kept getting better and better. Lots of people heard about this child wonder, and came to watch his matches.

Billy played in many matches all through his teen years, and seemed to get better and better. He was developing tricky spin shots and clever strategies that seemed to confuse his opponents. Billy's only problem was that it seemed to take him forever to get going. In the early part of his matches he seemed to be a little slow, and he often missed shots that everyone knew he could make with ease. By the middle of a match he was doing fine, but by this point he would be trying to play catch-up if he had fallen behind in the score. He even ended up losing matches that he should have won.

Billy and his coaches decided that the problem was due to the fact that he was a slow starter, and needed more time to warm up. Instead of only warming up with his opponent right before a match, Billy started coming to the tennis court an hour or two ahead of time, and going through a heavy workout with another player. This turned out to be the perfect solution, because Billy was now fully warmed up and ready to play when the real match started. He was back to his old self again, and tougher to beat than ever.

You can learn a good lesson from Billy. If you want to be prepared for your next class, then you need to finish your homework assignments *before* you attend it. If you don't, you will probably have a hard time understanding what your teacher is saying, you won't be able to answer your teacher's questions (which sure doesn't look good!), and you will find yourself falling behind.

Teachers usually give two different types of homework assignments: written assignments and reading assignments. From your written assignments, the teacher will know right away how much work you have done and how well you have understood the lesson. Although the teacher may not find out immediately how much you have understood from a reading assignment, this homework is just as important if you are to learn the subject. Reading assignments will determine how much you understand from your teacher's presentations in class, and how well you will do in the course.

As a student, your first job is to find out what the teacher expects from you in the way of homework assignments. Most teachers write the homework assignment that is due for the next day on the blackboard. Some will even write the assignments for the entire week on the board, both to let students know where the course is heading and also to allow them to work a little ahead if they wish. Make sure that you understand exactly what the teacher wants you to do; ask a question right then and there if you are unclear. Write down the homework assignment in your notebook rather than trying to remember it by heart.

Some instructors even pass out an outline of the course that covers a month or maybe the entire grading period. Such outlines may list all of the reading and written assignments and when they are due, and give you an even better idea of where the course is going. An outline like this is very helpful to students, because it allows them to prepare a schedule well in advance.

As you progress through school, you will find that many teachers use an outline to list all of the books and articles that you will be expected to read for the course. The list might include your textbooks for the course, as well as any extra books that the teacher would like for you to read. Your textbooks are the main books for the course, and are special because your teacher or the school feels that they contain a very good discussion of the subject. You should become very familiar with your textbooks because many teachers follow them closely when putting together their class presentations and homework assignments.

If the teacher has listed other books to read, then you should try to get hold of them even if they are not required for the course. The teacher has probably included these readings because they add to something that was either not covered, or not covered well, in your textbook. You might be able to find these other books in the library, or you might even buy them if you can find them in a bookstore. As I mentioned earlier, one of my hobbies is collecting books, and I feel very comfortable with books that I have read in detail.

What is important is not that you buy books, but that you actually read them. Here is some good advice on this from Mark Twain, one of our most famous American authors, who wrote *The Adventures of Tom Sawyer*, among many other books. He said, "The man who does not read good books has no advantage over the man who can't read them."

You should be in no doubt about when to read your books. As you can tell from the title of this chapter, you should do your reading assignment *before* you go to your next class. If that is the only thing that you get out of this chapter, then the chapter will have been a success.

When you do your reading assignment before going to class, you become more familiar with the subject, which makes it easier to understand your teacher's presentation in class. By knowing something about the subject ahead of time, your teacher's presentation will be more interesting and exciting because you can relate to it. You will also be a more active listener in class because you already know something about the subject. It is much easier to understand a subject the second time around, because you have already figured out some of the questions and problems from your first reading.

If you still have questions about the subject after your first reading, then the classroom is an excellent place to ask them. You can bring your questions up before, during, or after class, depending upon when your teacher prefers students to ask questions.

By speaking up when you have a question, you will let the teacher know that you have been thinking about the subject. Besides, if you have done your reading ahead of time, you should be able to answer many of the questions that the teacher asks in class. This will show that you are prepared and intelligent.

It is important for students to understand that they should do reading assignments for a purpose, and that purpose is to understand a subject. If you did not fully understand your reading assignment from the first reading, then you can go back and read it again if necessary. If you do this, it is still important to do the reading *before* the next class in which the teacher will discuss the subject. You should not go back and read the assignment after class, because you will start falling behind in your subjects.

I can remember from my school days that some students marked up their books to help them understand what they were reading. They would use pencil or magic marker to highlight the parts that they wanted to read again later to prepare for a test. You should not be marking up books that belong to the school because you will have to pay for them later. If you want to mark up your own books that is your choice, but I think it is better to write some notes on a separate piece of paper. Books that are marked up always look to me as if they are ruined. The important thing is not how much you can memorize from a book, but how much you have learned.

Don't think for a minute that you can take a shortcut around your reading assignments and still be a top student. Some students think that they can skip the reading assignments altogether if they can understand what the teacher says in class. The problem with this thinking is that you need to do the reading assignment first in order to understand all of what the teacher says in class.

Another important point is that there is more to a subject than what the teacher says in class. Your teacher probably does not have time to discuss everything about a subject in the classroom, only the more significant parts. The readings may contain some very interesting material that you need to understand if you are to master the subject. The only way to get it all is to put in the time and do the readings.

Most of the classes that you take in school will have some written homework assignments. These help you to continue to learn at home, and will tell your teacher if you are making good progress. This is especially true of courses in mathematics and the sciences. In these subjects you learn by doing, and you cannot go forward to the next step until you master the previous one.

Watching your teacher solve problems on the board in class will not necessarily teach you how to solve problems. You have to roll up your sleeves, use your head, get your hands a little dirty, and make some mistakes on your own by trying to solve the problems. Your goal should be to make the mistakes before a test, such as when you are doing your homework, so you will know the right way to solve problems when you take the test.

Many teachers collect homework assignments, grade them, and then return them to their students. It is very important that you do these assignments— and do them on time!—both to let your teacher know that you are doing the work, and to allow yourself to progress at the right rate. If you do not do your homework assignments on time, you will quickly find yourself falling behind, and it will be that much more difficult to catch up later on. Just remember that you should always turn in the homework due for a course, even if it is late. Homework can be a significant part of your total grade.

It is very important for students to have the right attitude about homework. Understand that homework is not something that teachers hand out to punish students; it is assigned to help students learn more about a subject. Once you understand this, you should be able to do your homework with more energy and enthusiasm.

If you come across something in a homework assignment that you do not understand, then ask the teacher to explain it to you. Asking questions shows your teachers that you are making an effort to learn the subject, which is why they assigned the homework in the first place. It is important for you to know the answers, because questions similar to those in the homework may actually appear on a test.

Here are a few tips that will help you do homework more efficiently and effectively. As soon as you get home from school, think about the homework assignments that you need to complete before the next class. It may help to write these down on a piece of paper so you can see the full extent of what you need to do. Then think about the order in which you will do them, and how much time you will spend on each one. Sometimes this is enough to get you started. The sooner you start, the quicker everything will be done. Don't procrastinate!

RECAP

Complete your homework before class, so you will:

1. be prepared for the next class,

2. understand more of the teacher's lecture,

3. turn in assignments on time,

4. ask and answer good questions in class.

Take Notes During Class

(. . . so you will become an active listener!)

Amy learned how to play chess from her older brothers. It started out as curiosity, but after learning how to move each of the chess pieces on the board, she became more and more interested in how the game is played. She liked the idea of two armies fighting against each other, and how you could use different approaches to trap or trick the person you were playing against. Amy would sit for hours and watch her brothers play, and she learned many of the moves that they used when playing each other.

Amy's brothers allowed her to play in some of the games with them and their friends. She quickly learned that it is much more difficult to play a game yourself than to watch someone play and figure out what they are doing. No matter how hard she tried, Amy was not able to win a single game against her brothers or their friends. After a while, she became so frustrated that she was ready to give up chess for good. In fact, she did give up the game for several months, until something unusual happened.

Some new neighbors moved into the vacant house across the street, and it turned out that they knew a lot about the game of chess. The family came from Russia, and the father had been a well-known chess expert there before coming to this country. Amy made friends with the new girl from Russia, and her father gave both of them lessons every day in how to play the game. He used strange words and phrases for his moves, such as the "Queen's Gambit," the "French Defense," and the "Sicilian Defense."

Amy listened to the instructions very carefully, but it was all so complicated that she had a hard time remembering what to do. The Russian champion showed Amy how to write abbreviations for the moves, and told her to take notes. Amy carefully wrote down everything she learned, and even tried the moves out on a computerized chess game at home.

The next time her brothers had their friends over, Amy challenged all of them to a chess tournament. After making a smart remark about how she should have learned her lesson before, they reluctantly agreed to play with her. The most difficult thing Amy had to do in the match was to hold in her laughter as they fell into her well-laid traps. The boys were having so much trouble playing her individually that she played them all at once. After she tore them up and they asked what she had been doing, Amy replied, "Oh, just watching you guys play."

. . .

Amy had learned a very good lesson from her chess instructor. When you are trying to learn something complicated, it is much easier to learn and remember if you take notes. She decided to use the same approach in her classes at school. At first Amy started taking notes in her science and math classes, since they were the most difficult, but after a while she took notes in all of her classes. She realized that she was not only understanding more of what the teacher said during class, but also remembering more when she left class.

If you go into just about any college class, you will find that most if not all of the students are taking notes. They know that taking good notes is one of the keys to making good grades. If you go into just about any class of younger students, you probably will find that few, if any, are taking notes. Younger students have not learned the importance of taking notes, and many do not know how to take them.

You must listen carefully to your teachers during class and take detailed notes if you have any hope of becoming a straight-A student. This is one of the main steps in my study system. You should try to capture everything important that your teachers present in class, because they may test you on this material. To do this, you must listen carefully, concentrate deeply, and have a good system for writing down what you have learned. If you obtain little or nothing during class, then you will not get a good grade in the course—it's that simple! The purpose of this chapter is to show you how to be a careful listener and a good note-taker.

Let's talk first about the ability to listen. Do you know how to tell a good listener from a poor listener?

The main characteristic of poor listeners is that they hear only what they want to hear. There are any number of factors that keep them from being good listeners. For example, they may not be interested in the subject, may not like their teacher, are bothered by noise in the classroom or the behavior of other students, or perhaps they just lack concentration. You must overcome any of these problems to become an effective listener.

If you have been doing the things we have already talked about, such as sitting in the front row and doing your assignments before class, then you are well on your way to becoming a better listener. More, however, is required.

Listening is different from reading, writing, or thinking, because another person is present. In order to be a good listener, you have to be a good follower. You will need to concentrate on what your teacher is saying, and avoid letting your mind drift off to other thoughts. This is more difficult than it sounds, because your brain can work several times faster than your teacher can speak. Use this advantage to think carefully about what the teacher is saying and to record it accurately in your notes.

If your teacher says something that you find really interesting, don't think too deeply about it at that point. There is plenty of time after class for deep thoughts. The best approach is for you to accept temporarily what the teacher has said, and be a good follower.

However, it is important that you not accept blindly everything that your teacher says. Teachers are not perfect, and they make mistakes too. If your teacher says something that you do not understand, or that does not sound right, then ask a question about it.

You should try to be intelligent about asking questions in class. Ask a question if you really need help, but don't be so anxious to ask your question that you interrupt the teacher or cause a disturbance in class. Ask good questions that will help you—and maybe even other students in the class—understand the subject better. Don't ask questions only because you want to be heard!

Good listeners are very alert during their teachers' presentations, because they know that they may have only one chance to understand the message. This is very different from reading a book, because you can go over the same section in a book several times until you understand it. You must always be very alert while your teacher is talking in class, or you run the risk of missing something important that will appear later on a test.

The way to be very alert during class is to use all of your senses to gather information. Your eyes should move back and forth between the blackboard and your notebook, your ears should be listening to your teachers' words, and your mind should be trying to figure out what they mean. Your entire body should be working continuously to understand every thought and idea expressed in the classroom. When you become this involved, you are less likely to drift off in a daydream.

The way to become a good listener is to take good notes, and the way to take good notes is to be a good listener. In other words, being a good listener and taking good notes go hand in hand.

The first rule for good note-taking is to bring all of the necessary supplies to class. You should have a well-organized notebook with plenty of paper, and also several sharpened pencils, erasers, pens, and other supplies (rulers, compasses, and so forth). I always preferred to take my notes in pencil so I could erase parts that I wanted to change.

Take *detailed* notes. You should be writing almost continuously so you can capture everything important that your teacher says in class. Forget about writing down the small stuff, such as unrelated stories, jokes, and so forth. Try to write down exactly what your teacher says, although you can do some translation into your own words if that makes the idea easier to understand. Be careful not to get so concerned about translation that you miss the teacher's next thought!

When it comes to studying for a test, you will find that your notes are only as good as the information that has gone into them; therefore, you need to be very careful in what you write. Be sure to copy everything into your notes that the teacher presents, such as graphs, charts, and tables. If your teacher tells you to organize the information into an outline, and writes one on the blackboard, make sure that it appears in your notes. Don't become so concerned, however, about creating your own outline that you miss what the teacher is saying.

It is just about impossible for anyone to write down every word that someone else says, unless they know shorthand and write very fast. I have a different approach for you to consider. When I was in school taking notes, I used abbreviations that I could figure out later on. This allowed me to write very fast, and capture everything important that the teacher presented.

There are several different things that you can do to abbreviate your writing. The first is to use standard abbreviations that mean just about the same thing to everybody. Some of the words you can abbreviate in this way include "for example" (e.g.); "equals" (=); "does not equal" (≠); "and" (&); "with" (w/); and "without" (w/o).

Another thing you can do for fast note-taking is to create your own abbreviations. You might abbreviate words by using the first few and last few letters in the word. You can also leave out vowels and use contractions where possible. For example, you might use the abbreviation "gov't" for the word "government." Try always to use the same abbreviations for words, so you will be able to figure out what they mean later on.

Finally, you can speed up your note-taking by writing shortened rather than complete sentences. In your notes, you might leave out parts of speech such as prepositions, conjunctions, and other words that are not absolutely necessary to understand an idea. You need to be very careful, however, not to leave out words that change the meaning of a thought.

I recommend that you *leave plenty of white space on the page* when taking notes. As you will see in the next step, you will be filling in all of your abbreviations and adding some more thoughts of your own. Having enough space makes this easier to do.

Now that you will be taking all of these notes, you will need a good system for organizing them. Always write down the date at the beginning of each class, and number the pages so you can keep track of them. This

is especially important if you are using a loose-leaf notebook, so you can put pages back in their proper place if
need to remove them. In your notebook, make a note of
your homework assignments, what they involve, and
when they are due.

It is very important to keep a neat notebook. Use
dividers in your notebook—and label them—to separate
the pages for each of the subjects you are taking. It can
be very confusing if papers from different subjects get
mixed up. Also, clean and rearrange your notebook regularly so it does not become too thick and awkward.

As you take notes in class, you should try to figure
out possible exam questions. If you are very alert, you
may notice a change in your teachers' movements or
voices when they are talking about an important idea or
fact. If a teacher gets very excited about a particular
subject, there is a good chance that it may show up on a
test. Some teachers will come right out during class and
tell you that certain subjects would make good questions
on a test. Make sure that you record this in your notes.

The fact is that teachers give hints, and sometimes
they give them over and over again. Always be on the
alert for hints. If you can figure out the exam questions
ahead of time, this will give you a big advantage
over your classmates. You will be able to collect your
thoughts and prepare a good answer before the test.

As a student, you should recognize that different
teachers have different styles of presenting information
in class. Some will hand out an outline—or write one on
the blackboard—listing the material they plan to cover
during class. Other teachers number their points, or repeat them several times for emphasis. Still others hand

out written summaries of the material they have covered during class. Recognizing your teachers' styles will help you get more out of your classes because you will know what to expect.

The fact is that it takes a lot of energy and effort to learn. When you take detailed notes, you will find that your body and mind are working almost every second that you are in class. As you become more involved, time passes very quickly and you become less aware of all of the work you are doing. After a while you become more excited as you learn more about a subject. The entire learning experience becomes more fun, and you start to look forward to your next class. You will enjoy being a few steps ahead of your classmates and, sometimes, even the teacher!

It takes a lot of hard work to become a good student, so you should not look for an easy way out. For example, don't think that you can use a tape recorder and skip taking notes in class. You will probably be less likely to listen to your teacher because you know that you can listen to the tape recorder later on. It is difficult to make much sense out of a tape recording when the teacher is referring to something on a blackboard that you can't see. You will always understand and remember more about a subject if you write it down immediately after you hear about it.

One last point: Even if you can understand everything that your teacher says in class, this does not mean that you do not have to take notes. There is no guarantee that you will be able to remember what the teacher said later on. The only way you can be certain is to take very detailed notes. This may be a lot of hard work but, as the famous American inventor, Thomas Edison, said, "There is no substitute for hard work."

RECAP

To take good notes during class:

1. bring proper supplies,

2. be an active listener and follower,

3. write down everything of importance,

4. use abbreviations liberally,

5. look for potential exam questions.

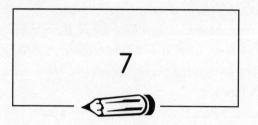

7

Review Your Notes Before the Next Class

(. . . it's never too soon to start studying!)

Mark is a complete football player. He plays quarterback, and is very skilled at passing, running, and carrying out plays. Everyone thinks he is brilliant, the way he mixes up his calls and marches his team up and down the field to score points. What most people do not realize is that Mark is not calling the plays. His coach over on the sideline is sending in each play with new players who enter the game. Mark still has a lot of responsibility, however, because he must recognize the play and successfully carry it out.

Mark faces a big challenge—probably the biggest in his career. There is less than one minute left in the last quarter of a playoff game, the score is 35-31, and Mark's team is the one that is behind. The offense on the other team has been very strong, and Mark's defense has been unable to slow them down. Now it's do or die—everything is on the line. Mark's team has the ball on the other team's seven-yard line, and it is third down. A field goal won't do it, since it is only three points, so they have to go for the touchdown.

The coach sends in the play, and Mark instantly recognizes it. Everyone is thinking pass, and this play calls for a pass, but it is a tricky one. Mark sends all of his eligible receivers into the far reaches of the end zone, except for one. A halfback stays in the backfield to block, giving Mark enough time to find a receiver. After Mark calls his signals and the ball is hiked, everyone carries out their assignment. The defensive players take the bait and cover all of the receivers. Just as it looks as though everything is lost, the lone halfback jogs across the line into the end zone and Mark tosses him a soft pass, which he catches. It almost looks too easy. The other team is unable to come back, and Mark's team wins the game.

After the game and all of the congratulations, Mark's coach remarks that the thing he is most impressed with is that Mark never missed a call. Many people do not realize that the game of football can be very complicated. Among the huge number of plays in the book, Mark had to instantly recognize a call and successfully carry it out. If he missed the call, or couldn't remember how to carry it out, the down would be blown and there might even be a turnover.

Mark confesses later to the coach that he has a secret for remembering all of the plays. Not only did he take careful notes when the coach was discussing the plays in the training room, before the next meeting he carefully went over his notes so he could understand and remember them. He made corrections to his notes and added his own thoughts, to make them clearer and easier to remember. If anything was still unclear, he asked the coach about it before the next meeting. By the day of the big game, everything was firmly in place.

His experiences with football have convinced Mark that the same strategy will work in the classroom. Not only does he take very careful notes in all of his classes, he reviews his notes *before* the next class. As with his football preparation, he makes corrections, adds his own thoughts, and discusses any problems with his teachers. Guess what? Mark is marching up and down the field in his school classes as well, and is a straight-A student. It almost looks too easy to his classmates but, as with football, everything works because of all of the preparation that goes in up front.

The lesson is clear: If you are going to understand everything that your teacher says in class, not only do you have to take good notes, you also have to review and correct them before the next class so you can learn at the same rate that the teacher presents new information. There is no other way!

Taking and reviewing notes is so important that I tell college students to *completely rewrite* their notes before their next class. Many college students only have class in a particular course a couple of times a week, so it is possible for them to do this. Students in elementary, middle, and high school usually have class every day, so they would not have time to rewrite all of their notes. That is why I tell these students to *review and correct* their notes before the next class.

Shortly after you attend a class, find a quiet spot where you can really concentrate on what you have written in class. As you review your notes, you should be rethinking the material that your teacher presented in class. If you have made any abbreviations in your notes, you should be filling them out with complete thoughts and sentences. As part of the process, you should correct anything in your notes that is incomplete or inconsistent.

Many students find that it helps them to add an outline to their notes. This is not to say that you should rearrange what your teacher said in class, only that you should add headings that outline the structure of your teacher's message. As you do this, make sure that you can distinguish major points from minor details.

It also helps for students to add their own thoughts and comments to their notes. This not only makes it easier to understand information, it is very helpful if you are asked to express an opinion on a subject during an exam. Just make sure that you can identify and separate your own comments from those of your teachers.

You should have enough room to add all of this extra information if you left plenty of white space on the page when taking your original notes, as I recommended in the last chapter.

Make sure that you really understand what you have written. In an earlier chapter I talked about the importance of being an active reader. You should also review your notes in an active manner, by asking questions about the meaning and importance of your teacher's statements, and thinking about which of them might be good test questions.

If there is something in your notes that you just cannot figure out on your own, then make a point to ask your teacher about it either before or during the next class. You might be able to visit your teacher after school that day, or before school begins on the next day, to get an answer to a particularly difficult problem. By doing this, you will be able to keep up with your teacher's lesson, and your teacher will know that you are a serious student who really wants to learn.

By reviewing your notes, and correcting and filling them in, you will be reinforcing what you have learned.

The main reason for reviewing your notes *before* the next class is to start studying for the test. You can never start too soon in studying for a test. Most students complain that they do not have enough time to study, and it is usually because they started too late!

It may take you a little more time in the short run to review notes, but it should take less time in the long run when you actually review them for a test. Your understanding will be greater because you have already mastered the material, and the review will be much easier and more comfortable. You will also have more confidence, because you are just reviewing what you already know.

It will take some discipline for you to review your notes before the next class, and still get your reading assignment done. You will need to spend your time wisely; after a while, you will probably develop a system of what to study when. It is possible to get everything done on time, and still have plenty of time left over to do all of the other things you want to do.

If you really want to be a straight-A student, then you need to follow all of the steps I am describing. If you skip any of the steps, then you are not really following my system. Reviewing your notes *before* the next class is essential!

Let me give you some evidence that is convincing. Experiments have shown that average people remember only about twenty percent of what they read, forty percent if they hear it after reading it, and sixty percent if they also write it. So consider this: By reviewing and filling in your notes, you will be able to understand and remember much more than sixty percent.

The rest of the steps I will present will show you how to raise your level of understanding as close to the hundred percent mark as possible.

RECAP

To review your notes *before* the next class:

1. organize your notes,

2. fill in missing information and abbreviations,

3. check with the teacher to clear up inconsistencies,

4. you have already started studying for the test!

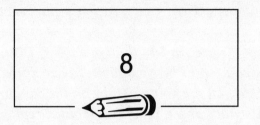

8

Prepare for Tests Ahead of Time

(. . . by studying a week in advance.)

Denise had lived in the inner city all of her life, and had never been on an overnight camping trip. Then, one day near the end of the term, her school announced that they were offering students the opportunity to go for a one-week hiking and camping trip to the Appalachian mountains. The school would supply the tents, sleeping bags, backpacks, cooking utensils, and food. Students would be responsible for everything else. The price was very reasonable, and several of Denise's friends planned to go, so she decided to join the party.

When Denise went to school the next day, she told Mrs. Rogers, her home economics teacher, about her plans to go on the trip. Mrs. Rogers was always talking about things to do around the house, so perhaps, Denise thought, she would have some good tips for getting along in the outdoors. Their conversation went something like this:

"School is over in less than one week, Denise," noted Mrs. Rogers, "and I bet you haven't even started to think about what you are going to take on the camping trip."

"But what's there to think about?" replied Denise. "The school is supplying just about everything we will need: tents, sleeping bags, backpacks, food, and so on. It sounds like all we have to do is show up."

"Are you kidding!" exclaimed Mrs. Rogers. "I was a Girl Scout leader for many years, and I can tell you that you will need everything you use at home, and a lot more!"

"Well, I know I have to bring my clothes," said Denise, with a puzzled look on her face, "but what else are you talking about?"

Mrs. Rogers then started to list a huge number of items that Denise hadn't even thought of. "How many changes of clothes will you need? And don't forget about a fresh change of underclothing and socks for each day. And what about wash rags, towels, and soap, and don't forget that you will want to put on some makeup when you get up in the morning. And if you don't want to look into the bottom of a pot, you had better take your own mirror. What about personal-care items, like fingernail clippers, or extra blankets if it gets cold at night—the mountains can get pretty cold at night. What about a first-aid kit, in case you have an accident?" And the list went on, and on, and on. . . .

By this time Denise was getting a little worried. Right after she got home from school that day, she made up her own list. Then she got a backpack from the school, and started packing. By the time the camping trip rolled around, she was ready to go. When she actually got to the camp site, Denise realized that she had not thought of everything, but she was way ahead of everyone else. She thought to herself, "Thank you, Mrs. Rogers!"

The behavior that helped Denise get ready for her camping trip is the same behavior that will help you succeed in the classroom. Too many students think that they can wait until the last day to start studying for a test, and then cram everything in at the last minute. By this time it is too late! A one-week period, like Denise used to get ready for a trip, is a good amount of time to start preparing for a test. If your teacher does not give you this much time, you should at least start studying several days in advance.

You may not realize it, but you have probably been studying for a test much longer than a week if you have been following my study system up to this point. By doing your reading assignments ahead of time, and taking careful notes and reviewing them, you have mastered information as your teacher presented it to you. This does not, however, mean that you are ready to take a test without doing anything else.

After a while, the ideas and facts that you know begin to get a little hazy, even though they were very clear when you first learned them. Even though they may still be in your memory, the longer the time since your last test, the weaker your understanding is likely to be. That is why everyone, no matter how good a student they are, needs to review their notes and reading materials before taking a test. There is no other way around it!

Most teachers announce the dates of their tests well in advance to give students plenty of time to study for them. Some teachers hand out a schedule at the beginning of the term, or write the dates of tests on the blackboard. This will help you plan your study schedule very carefully. If your teacher has not provided this information, then you may want to go up and ask about it.

I know that some teachers like to give unannounced tests, or "pop quizzes" as they are called, to make sure that students are keeping up with their studies. I have had a few teachers who would do this, and I can tell you that I definitely did not like it. Pop quizzes always seemed like something of a dirty trick to me. But even if your teacher does this, you will be more prepared than the other students if you have been following my system, because you will be studying as you go.

To prepare for an announced test, you will need to review your notes from class, as well as any reading materials that the teacher mentions. Reading your notes from class should be painless, because you have already reviewed them, made corrections, and filled them in so they are easier to understand. The information is already in your mind. All you need to do is review the material so you will have control over it. Once you have control over the material, you will have control over the test.

When reviewing reading materials, think carefully about what you need to review. You probably do not need to go back and reread everything, particularly if the reading assignments were very long. Sometimes you can get by with making up an outline of the readings. In many courses, such as English, social studies, mathematics, and science, you will have been answering questions at the end of each section that test your knowledge. Many times, all you need to do is review your answers to these questions, and perhaps glance through the chapter so you can remember what was in it. On the other hand, if your teacher tells you to reread a chapter because it will be important on a test, then you had better do it.

As I said earlier, it is good to start your review one week, or at least several days, in advance. Pick up your notes, and any questions or problems you answered, and start your first review. If you don't finish reading all of this information on the first day, then you can pick up where you left off on the next day. In this first reading, don't try to memorize and relate all of the complicated information. The idea of this first reading is to refresh your memory, and build up your confidence that you have a basic understanding of the material that will be covered on the test.

The best way to understand information is to reread it several times, and think deeply about it. After finishing the first review of your notes and other materials, you should have several days left before the test. Take a short break, and then begin your second review of the materials.

Your second review should be much more active than your first. Make sure that you can clearly identify major and minor points, and also understand important definitions. One good way to get command over information is to recite (repeat out loud) the details of a subject during your review.

As an example, suppose you think you might be asked on a test to recite the first ten amendments (the Bill of Rights) to the U.S. Constitution. Unlike the earlier example I used, which required only knowledge of the First Amendment, the answer to this question requires a substantial amount of memorization. To prepare yourself for this question, you will probably need to recite the first ten amendments several times to yourself.

If you are still having trouble remembering the details, try to relate them to something you know about. In fact, try to relate the information to something you have actually experienced, because this makes it even easier to remember. Sometimes it is possible to identify a few key words that will help you remember a whole lot more about a subject.

Your second review of your study materials should be much easier than the first. During the second review, you should almost be able to guess the order of the ideas, because the information is still fresh in your mind from the first reading. At this point, you should start to feel that you are getting command of the information, so you can use it any way you want to answer test questions. This should make you more comfortable with the information, and build your self-confidence.

After finishing your second review, take another short break and then begin your third review. By this time you should almost be able to guess what is on the

next page of your notes or reading materials before looking at them. Even more important, you should now be
able to look at information in different sections of your
notes and reading materials and see relationships between them. This is very important, because teachers
like to ask questions on tests that require you to relate
and compare information. You should now feel that you
can do this, and may even look forward to the test so
you can show your teacher what you have learned.

You should always try to review your notes and reading materials three times to prepare for a test. I don't
think it is necessary to do more than this, unless you
find the subject particularly difficult. After a certain
point you will not get as much benefit from the additional reviews because you already will have a good understanding of the subject. On the other hand, if you only
do one or two reviews, you might not have mastered the
subject, and may do poorly on the test.

There is an old English saying that goes as follows:

Multiplication is vexation,
Division is as bad;
The rule of three doth puzzle me,
And practice drives me mad.

By the way, the word "vexation" refers to something that
really bothers you. Whether you are puzzled by the "rule
of three," or even if "practice drives [you] mad," you are
going to have to face up to the fact that you will need to
review your study materials three times before a test to
get top marks. This is the only way to do it!

Here are some other rules that will help you prepare for tests while you are reviewing your study materials:

1. Think about the questions that your teacher might ask. This is not as difficult as it may sound, because the information you learn in a subject can usually be grouped into major categories. After you have reviewed your study materials three times, you should be able to figure out the major categories.

Here is an approach that always worked for me. After your review, make up some possible test questions and think about how you would answer them. Think about how to organize your information in order to write the best answer. By rehearsing in this way, you will have a better understanding of the information, and you'll be able to remember it for a longer period of time. This will also give you good practice in expressing yourself, which is what you will be asked to do on a test. This useful drill will help you prepare for the real test.

2. Rewrite certain mathematical equations, graphs, and charts. Subject such as mathematics and science use a lot of equations, formulas, graphs, charts, and symbols. Reading them over three times may not be enough to make you really comfortable with the information. Sometimes the best way to get familiar with equations and charts is to write them several times, so you will know them by heart. If you are still having trouble, you can glance at them every now and then, right up to the day of the test, if necessary. This will give you practice, and build your self-confidence.

3. Pay attention to materials that your teacher hands out in class. Many teachers hand out extra materials in class, both on subjects that are very complicated, and subjects that they did not have time to cover in class.

You should give any handouts the same importance as if the teacher had actually covered the material in class. Review these materials carefully, and make any notes that will help you understand them better. It is especially important for you to understand any relationship between the material in the handout and the material that your teacher covered in class. This type of information has a way of showing up on test, so it is wise to be prepared.

4. Memorize information if necessary. There are some courses in school in which it is important to remember key dates, formulas, equations, and so forth. In most cases, you can probably remember these from your normal review of the notes and reading materials. But sometimes more is required. The biggest problem is that most students do not know how to memorize information.

Flash cards can be a very helpful tool. Write the information that you want to remember on a three-by-five-inch index card. I like to write the idea or word on the front of the card, and the detailed information that I want to remember on the back of the card. Then, when I have some extra time, I can glance at the front of the card and see if I can remember what is on the back. You can do this as often as you want, until everything is part of your memory.

5. Review information in a steady and organized way. The key to a successful study program is to begin your review well in advance, and continue studying during the period leading up to the test. It is best to try and study something every day, or at least every other day, rather than putting your study materials aside for several days. In this way you can get control over information more quickly, because you do not have to go back and remember where you left off. It is wise to use a calendar, so you can keep track of how you are spending your time.

6. Never study up to the last minute before a test. If possible, you should finish your studying the day before—or at least, a few hours before—the big test. Studying up to the last minute can create a lot of pressure. To do really well on a test, you need to be rested, calm, and mentally ready. Rest is very important, and you should make a point of getting plenty of sleep the night before a big test.

If you decide to join a study group, just be sure that you join a group of students who will work hard and have something to contribute, rather than expecting you to do all of the work for them.

My main piece of advice is that if you want to do well on exams, then you have to study for them. There is no other way around it. Don't think for a minute that you can walk into a test with an empty head and get lucky on guessing the questions and answers. If you have an empty head, then you are probably going to get an empty score.

RECAP

To prepare for tests ahead of time:

1. start studying a week, or several days, in advance,

2. review your lecture notes three times,

3. think about potential exam questions,

4. conduct your review in an organized manner,

5. never study up to the last minute.

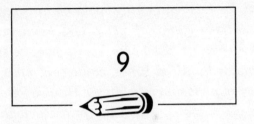

Be Testwise and Confident

(. . . because confidence breeds success!)

Though Nick is an all-around baseball player, his real specialty is hitting. He has almost a .500 batting average, which means that he gets a hit about one time for every two times at bat. Fifty percent is a failing mark in school, but in baseball it puts you at the top of the heap. In fact, Nick is even better than his numbers indicate. Nick's coach calls him a "money hitter," which means that he gets a hit when you really need it—like right at the end of the game when you need a hit to win!

You are probably wondering, "How did Nick get so good? Was he born that way?" Not at all. In fact, Nick used to be a less-than-average hitter. It was only when he learned how to hit that he became so good. "So," you probably want to know, "what's Nick's secret?"

Like anyone who is very good at anything, Nick works

very hard. He has read many books on hitting, and gone to many hitting camps to get professional instruction. Every day when he gets home from school he swings the bat at least a hundred times, so he can move his arms like a piece of precision machinery. He also joins baseball teams every season so he can practice what he has learned.

All of the hard work has made Nick a good hitter, but this is not the real secret for his great hitting. Nick is a serious student of the game of baseball. He carefully watches different pitchers to see what they can throw: fastball, change-up, curveball, slider, and so forth. Nick knows that different pitchers like to work in different ways, so he studies the order in which they throw their pitches. For example, if a pitcher gets two strikes in a row on you, does he come back at you with a curveball or a change-up?

When Nick gets up to bat he tries to get inside the pitcher's mind. In the on-deck circle, he practices swings with each throw to make sure that he has the pitcher timed. When Nick steps up to the plate, he tries to figure out the type of pitch and its location, and then in his own mind, he sees himself hitting the ball exactly where he wants. Nick doesn't guess right all of the time, but he guesses right often enough to make him a .500 hitter. This has given him a lot of confidence that he can keep doing it in the future.

Nick has had such good success in hitting baseballs that he has decided to use a similar approach in the classroom. He tries to figure out the test questions ahead of time, so he will be prepared for whatever the teacher throws at him. As with baseball, Nick cannot guess what the questions will be all of the time, but he guesses correctly often enough that he is very confident he will do well on a test. The result is that Nick's grade-point average is much higher than his .500 batting average on the baseball field—he is batting near a thousand in the classroom!

In order to do well on tests you must know how to take them—you have to be "testwise." In an earlier chapter on "How to Take a Test," I reviewed the basic methods for taking various types of tests, such as essays, multiple-choice, true-false, fill-in-the-blanks, and so forth. I am now going to assume that you are a testwise student, and I will describe more advanced methods, such as how to figure out the questions on a test and be confident that you can answer them. If you do not remember the skills from the chapter on "How to Take a Test," you should go back and read it at some point.

On tests, teachers like to ask students to use the methods that they have taught them in the classroom. These methods are like a bag of tools that a worker might use, in the way that a carpenter might use a saw and hammer to build a house. You will need to know what tools to use on particular problems, and how to use them. This will be especially true in courses such as science and math, where you will need to know how to use different equations and formulas to solve problems.

The first rule when taking tests is to have a completely open mind. Even though you have thought about the likely test questions beforehand, don't try to force your answer into the exact question you thought would be asked. Your teacher may be asking you to apply your knowledge in a different way. The really challenging tests force you to move out of your ordinary way of thinking, and come up with something creative.

If you started studying for a test several days ahead of time, and read your study materials three times, you will have loaded a lot of information into your mind. Your mind will be working with all of this information in the days before the test, going over the various facts, ideas, and relationships. This should put you in a good, creative mood for taking the test.

In order to get the most out of your creativity, you should go into a test with the right attitude and a lot of self-confidence. Try to think of a test as an opportunity to show your teacher just how much you have learned. If you have been following my study system, you should have peace of mind, because your mind will be well-organized. If you are confident, you are more likely to do well because you will have the right attitude. It is what I referred to earlier as the "self-fulfilling prophecy"—if you think you will do well, then you will, and if you think you will do poorly, then you will!

If you play sports, then I am sure you have heard your coach talk about the importance of confidence during a game. Confidence helps athletes do their very best, and gain an advantage over their opponents. Taking a test is similar to playing a game because you are competing against the teacher and the other students in the class. The teacher is challenging you to answer a set of questions, and you are competing with other students to see how well you can do. In a sense, you are also competing with yourself, because you are trying to make your answer as good as possible. Whether in sports or school, always aim your sights high, and be confident that you can win!

The opposite feeling of confidence is fear. Many students are frightened to death at the thought of taking an exam. They get very nervous and worried about tests—and may even feel sick—because they are afraid they are going to fail. Then they start thinking about all of the terrible things that will happen to them if they do fail. They think about all of the criticism they will get from their parents, teachers, and even other students.

Many students get nervous about tests because they think they have a lot to lose. This is especially true of students who have studied very hard for a test, and want to get rewarded for their efforts. The very thought that they might do poorly on a test makes them nervous and worried. This is very unfortunate, because sometimes they become so nervous and worried that they cannot think during the test, and they actually bring about the thing they hoped to avoid.

Now, don't confuse the fear of failure with the desire to succeed. It is very natural to get worked up before a test. If you get a little excited, and get your juices going, this can actually help you do better on a test. It is very similar to an athlete getting worked up before a big game, and doing better because of the excitement. This is a very different emotion from fear.

The main reason that students become frightened about tests is that they lack self-confidence. Students who have done poorly on tests in the past, or who are not confident about the way they studied for a test, are the ones who will be the most nervous. If you are following my study methods, then you should be confident that you will do well on tests. As you experience success on tests you will become even more confident, because you will know that you have done everything possible to get a good grade.

If you have been afraid of taking tests in the past, how do you go about getting rid of this fear? After all, it is often difficult to change our feelings about something immediately. You will have a better attitude if you understand what tests are all about. A test is designed to measure your understanding of a subject, and show where you need improvement. They don't say anything about you as a person, such as how smart you are, only how much you know about a subject at a certain time. Sometimes tests are less threatening if you think about them in this way. You should never think less of yourself if you have done poorly on a test.

Tests are nothing but a learning tool for helping you and your teacher measure your performance and progress. It is important to realize that since we are all human beings, we are going to make mistakes. No one is perfect. I have made plenty of mistakes over my lifetime, and you will make plenty too. Your goal should be to make mistakes before the exam, learn from them, and avoid repeating them on the exam.

Most teachers review the correct answers to questions when they return tests to their students. If you have made mistakes on a test, make sure that you know where you went wrong so you will not repeat the same mistakes in the next test, or in the final, the next course, or later during your lifetime. We gain real intelligence by learning from our mistakes, and set the stage to learn even more in the future.

Tests also help you to learn some important things about your teachers. Although teachers do not necessarily ask the same questions in all of their classes, and may change the questions from year to year, they often ask the same type of questions. You should try to learn something about the types of questions your teachers like to ask.

After your teachers give their first tests, try to figure out each teacher's style. Did your teacher give an essay test, a multiple-choice or true-false test, or some other type of test? What types of questions did your teacher ask? Did your teacher want you to memorize facts, solve complicated problems, or understand the relationship between ideas? Were the questions very broad or very narrow? Understanding your teachers' styles can help you do better on the next test or the final exam.

You will have a better understanding of exams if you know how your teachers grade them. Most teachers give grades according to what in statistics is called the "normal distribution." In other words, only a few students will get the highest grades, more will be in the middle, and only a few will fail. Sometimes you will have a teacher who claims that everyone get either high or low grades, but usually the school forces them to have some kind of distribution. This means that you will have to work very hard for one of the few A's the teacher will give out.

When your teacher uses a distribution system

(grades on a "curve"), the grade you get reflects not only how much you have learned, but also how much your classmates know. If there are a number of smart students in your class, there will be a lot of competition for the top grades. On the other hand, if your class has a number of poor students, it will be easier for you to come out on top.

The way some teachers give grades is even more complicated than this. The grade you get may depend on the grades the teacher gave other students before he or she grades your test. This is particularly true on essay tests, where the teacher needs to look at a number of papers to get a feel for how well students answered the questions.

Your grades on tests will depend mainly on the things that your teacher thinks are important. Some teachers like to see that students understand ideas, and that they present their answers in an organized way. Some put a lot of emphasis on grammar, spelling, and handwriting. Still others are influenced by how much they think you know, based on your classroom participation. The most important thing is to find out as soon as possible what your teacher thinks is important. As you get more familiar with your teacher, you will know what to emphasize on tests.

I always advise students to concentrate on learning a subject rather than worrying about the grade. Usually, if you understand a subject, the good grades will follow. Sometimes, however, you may really understand a subject, but do poorly because things did not go right for you on a test. If you tried very hard to understand a subject, and put forth your best effort on the test, this by itself will give you some satisfaction—even if your grade was not as high as you had hoped! When I am coaching base-ball, I always tell my players after a loss that there will be plenty of other opportunities to show what they can do. It is the same with tests.

Now, I am not recommending that you should be sat-isfied with grades that are beneath your ability. You should always aim for the top and do your very best. What I *am* saying is that sometimes it takes a little time and practice to reach the very top. All you have to do is to be patient and stick with it—success will follow!

RECAP

To be testwise and confident:

1. **believe in yourself,**

2. **keep an open mind,**

3. **know your teacher's style,**

4. **apply what you know.**

Show What You Know on the Final Exam

(. . . because it's a big part of your final grade!)

Lori loves to figure skate. She put on her first pair of skates when she was only four years old, and her ankles bent and she tumbled onto the ice. It was a great accomplishment just to stand up straight. Now Lori is in her early teens, and is a rising young star. She can do a variety of spins, jumps, and complicated dance steps that make the audience say "oooh" and "aaah." Lori's dream is to be in the Olympics someday, where she can do even more difficult moves like the double axel and triple salchow.

Figure skating is one of the most difficult sports to master, and requires a tremendous amount of discipline. Lori spends hours and hours each day practicing her jumps, spins, and dance steps over and over again to perfect them. Many times she tries to go beyond what she was able to do before, and ends up on the ice, just like when she was very young. Even when she successfully completes a spin or jump, there is the question of form, and how it will look in competition and be graded by a judge.

Lori has a very excellent coach who spends several hours with her each day. The coach watches her like a judge, and seems to find something to complain about with almost every move. It's not that the coach thinks Lori is doing a poor job; it's just that she wants Lori to get as close to perfect as possible, so she will realize her full potential. She pushes Lori to do something she has never done before, and when Lori does it they work on perfecting the form. As the coach told Lori one day, "The secret to figure skating is repetition. To be really good you have to do something over and over again until it becomes so natural, you don't even have to think or worry about it."

One day Lori told her coach that it didn't seem fair that you could work so hard for years, and yet make a mistake and look bad in a big competition that lasts only minutes. The coach said that this is the nature of the sport, and that it why it is so important to practice very hard every day. Then Lori's coach gave her some good advice to help her skate better in competition: "When you are out there on the ice, don't think about the audience or the judges watching your every move. Block them out of your mind completely. Your only goal should be to show me, your coach, what you have learned and what you can do. In this way, it will be just like an ordinary practice."

. . .

The coach's advice to Lori in the ice rink also works very well in the classroom. Taking a big test is very much like competing in a big sporting event. You have been working very hard to prepare for a test, and everything is on the line. You shouldn't worry about all of the effort you have put into it, or how the teacher will grade your exam. Your goal should be to show your teacher how much you have learned.

Many teachers give a big test at the end of each quarter, or a final at the end of the school year. These exams often have a huge effect on your final grade because they are the last test given by the teacher. I even had some teachers in college who said that what you get on the final is what you get in the course. I think most teachers in elementary, middle, and high school will raise your grade if you do very well on a final. In a sense, the big test at the end measures how much you have learned about the subject.

Before you take a big test, the first thing you need to find out is what will be covered. Most teachers will tell you ahead of time what you will be responsible for on a test. Ask your teacher if the test will cover only information learned since the last test, or from the entire quarter or year. The answer to this question will determine how you should go about studying for the test.

If the test will cover only material learned since the last exam, then you should study for it like any other test. In other words, review your class notes and reading materials since the last exam, just as I have described in earlier chapters. On the other hand, if the test will cover the entire quarter or year, then you need to go back to the very beginning and review your study materials. This should not be too difficult because my study methods have been helping you to learn and remember information throughout the entire quarter or year.

One of the most difficult things about taking big tests at the end of the quarter or year is that you have a lot of work to do. This is the time when all of your teachers want to give their big tests. To get ready, you should take a close look at your schedule at least a couple of weeks before the end of the term to see when the exams will be given. You can then work your way back from each of the tests to find out when you need to begin studying. If your schedule is very busy and you have several tests, then you may need to start studying sooner than you would have started earlier in the term.

If you are studying for a final, then you should use a slightly different approach than for regular tests. Exams given at regular times usually test your knowledge and understanding of very specific subjects. On the other hand, exams given at the end of the term usually test your knowledge and understanding of the big themes and ideas that the teacher covered throughout the term.

As you review your study materials for a test at the end of the quarter or year, look for these big themes that seem to run through the various subjects you studied. This should not be too difficult if you have been following my study methods, because earlier preparation will have helped you to understand the various subjects and see how they fit together. Once you have identified the major themes, make sure that you have specific knowledge that goes under each of these themes.

To get ready for a big exam at the end of the quarter or year, it is a good idea to go back and review the tests you took earlier. Although your teacher probably won't ask the same questions on the final, the questions may be of a similar type and pattern. Make sure that you understand the complete answers to questions on these earlier tests, particularly if you missed all or part of them. Your goal should be to go into the big test with complete knowledge of everything the teacher presented during the term, so you won't make the same mistakes over again.

Sometimes it also helps if you can find out what questions the teacher asked on previous final exams. Some teachers keep a file of past tests, and make them available to students through the library. If these are not available, you might talk to students in the grade ahead of you, to see if they saved their old exams, or possibly remember some of the questions that the teacher asked.

Since it is unlikely that your teacher will ask the same questions again, when you look at previous exams, don't try to memorize or write complete answers to the questions. The main idea is to get a feel for the types of questions your teacher asks on final exams. For example, look at the number of questions, the kind of subjects they cover, whether they are essay or objective questions, and the time you have to answer them. You should have learned something about your teacher's style of asking questions from taking tests during the regular term, but he or she may decide to do something different on the final.

You need to be very careful about how you use your time to study at the end of the term, because it will slip away from you very quickly. Work very hard, but still allow time for breaks so you won't burn out. Think about some other activities that you can cut back on, and then reward yourself with them later after the big test is over.

You should not be concerned that the final is the biggest test of the year, and that it will have a major effect on your grade. Everything will fall into place if you take your final as you would any other test, and concentrate on doing your best.

RECAP

To make an A on your final exam:

1. know what material will be covered,

2. start studying well ahead of time,

3. look for major themes,

4. review previous exams,

5. show the teacher what you have learned.

WHAT YOU HAVE LEARNED

2. How to Make Straight A's
(. . . and have fun doing it!)

RULE 1
Take the right subjects.

RULE 2
Work with your teacher.

RULE 3
Never miss a class.

RULE 4
Always sit up front.

RULE 5
Complete your homework before class.

RULE 6
Take notes during class.

RULE 7
Review your notes before the next class.

RULE 8
Prepare for tests ahead of time.

RULE 9
Be testwise and confident.

RULE 10
Show what you know on the final exam.

3

Making It Work for You

(. . . by working smarter, not harder!)

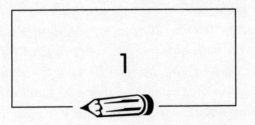

Develop Good Study Habits

(. . . by learning how to manage your time.)

When Ronnie steps out onto the basketball court, he is all business. He has spent hours every day on the basketball court for the past several years, starting with the neighborhood playground when he was so small that he could barely get both arms around the basketball. Ronnie is more comfortable on the basketball court than anywhere else in the world. Now he glides along the court almost without any effort, dribbles the ball so fast that you can barely see it, and makes long-distance shots from so far away that you have to think he has a built-in radar.

Ronnie needs everything he's got and more on the evening I am going to tell you about, because his team is one point behind with less than ten seconds left in the game, and they have to win to stay in the tournament. He even wore his favorite T-shirt for warm-ups before the game, which reads, "It's real simple—if you lose, you go home!" Everyone on both sides of the court figures that Ronnie will make the last shot, because he's got the highest shooting average on the team. And everyone knows that a basket will just about seal it for Ronnie's team.

Ronnie takes a pass from a teammate and starts dribbling it up the court. When he passes the half-court line, another player from the other team joins the action, his arms waving wildly in the air. Ronnie is aware of the seconds ticking off the clock, and for a moment thinks he can hear them in his ears, until he realizes that it is his heart pounding. When he is just outside the three-point line, he goes up for a jump shot, and the other two players go up with him. Realizing that it is a low-percentage shot, Ronnie makes a perfect side-arm pass to his teammate, who then does an easy lay-up for two points. The buzzer goes off, and Ronnie's team walks away with the win.

At practice the next day, Ronnie's coach pulls him aside and gives him the following advice: "Ronnie, that was a great move the other day. Your quick thinking helped us to win the game. Now I want you to do some more thinking about your subjects in school. If you don't keep your grades up, you're not going to be able to play basketball in this school, or later on in college. You're as comfortable on the basketball court as anyone I have ever known. Find a place just as comfortable to study at home, and put in the same kind of effort, and I'm sure everything will fall into line."

.   .   .

It's not enough to know something; you must actually practice it to become skilled. This is true whether you are on the athletic field or in the classroom. If you want to become a straight-A student, then you will need to practice the right study habits—and stay away from the wrong ones!

I had a teacher very early in my education who said that if you want to know everything about a subject, you need to ask yourself six questions; *who, what, where, when, how,* and *why?* I don't need to tell you *who* will be studying (you!), and by this point I shouldn't have to tell you *why!* Therefore, I will concentrate on the other four questions.

When to Study

As with sports, if you want to become a better student, then you should be doing something every day. This does not mean that you should be studying all day, or even studying the same amount each day. What it does mean is that you should at least try to accomplish something every day if you want to make progress in becoming a better student.

I am not in favor of filling out detailed calendars that describe what you are supposed to be doing during every second, minute, and hour of the day. This would be very boring, and you probably wouldn't be willing to follow it anyway. What I am in favor of is writing down *significant* dates on a calendar. For example, you should write down the dates for tests, or when papers are due, so you will have enough time to prepare for them.

Try to plan how you will use your time to study for at least a couple of days at a time. You should have a good idea of the work that will be required in each of your courses over the next couple of days. For example, you will probably need to review the notes you took in class, do some reading or writing assignments, prepare for one or more tests (if some are coming up), or do some other assignments. The idea is to use your time wisely so you can complete the work in all your classes, and still have time left over for other activities. By planning only a few days ahead at a time, you can make changes that will help you use your time very efficiently.

The way to make the best use of your time is to do your schoolwork during periods when there are no other activities that you want to participate in. If you have a big game or other event coming up, think about whether you can get in some studying right before or after the activity. If you know that you are going to very busy with some activity tomorrow, perhaps you should spend more time studying today.

The way you spend your time will depend mostly on the hours that you want to keep open for leisure. Some students like to take their leisure time right after they get home from school, and others would rather take it later in the evening. I would encourage you to start studying as soon as you get home from school, so you can get your work done and not have to worry about it or run short of time later on. Just remember that you need to have some leisure time every day, or you could burn yourself out. The best approach is to use leisure time as a reward for getting work done; that is why I put the work first.

Where to Study

Pick a spot where you feel very comfortable, can concentrate, and are able to get a lot of work done. Some students find that they can study best in a certain chair or room in their house. They feel very comfortable in this spot, and naturally think of it as a place to study. Other students may be more comfortable in the library, because of all of the books and other people studying. There is no single best spot for everyone—you need to decide what works best for you.

In order to use your time wisely, you should realize that there are many places to study other than your special place. For example, you could be thinking about the subjects you are studying while you are getting dressed in the morning, eating meals, waiting for or riding on the school bus, walking to class, or even going on a family trip. When you are with your classmates, either in school or out of school, there will be opportunities to discuss the subjects you are studying.

Wherever you decide to study, just remember that what is going on in your head is a lot more important than what is going on around you. If you are really interested in a subject, you can usually focus on it and ignore a lot of things going on around you, such as noise and other distractions. The power of concentration is an important one that will help you not only in school, but also at work and in everything else you do later on.

What to Study

By now you should have a good idea of the various things you need to do to become a good student. You know that you have to do your reading and writing assignments, review your notes, and prepare for all tests. Now it is important to know what subjects to study, and in what order, and also how much to study.

As soon as you sit down to do your studies each day, think about what you want to accomplish by the end of your study period. Think about the subject you will study first, and how much you will get done, then what you will do next, and so on for all your subjects. For ex- ample, think about the number of pages you will read for your history or civics class, the number of math or science problems that you will solve, or how many pages you will write for your English paper. Do your best to accomplish your goal. By working hard every day, and meeting your goals, you will have a sense of real accom- plishment.

It is always best to think about what you want to get done, rather than how long you will study. If you worry about how long to spend studying each subject, you may end up watching the clock and getting less done. As you think about what you want to accomplish, be very real- istic. Don't set goals that are so ambitious that you have no chance of accomplishing them, because this can be very frustrating.

As you think about the order of subjects to study, try to add some variety to make your work interesting. For example, if you spend a lot of time solving complicated math or science problems, you could follow this up by reading a chapter in your English or history book. It is also a good idea to mix subjects you like with those you are not wild about. For example, if you are not crazy about science but love English, you might read a novel after finishing your science assignment. By mixing your subjects in this way, you will be able to study longer without getting bored or tired.

Some students say they are only going to work hard in the subjects they like, and forget the rest, but this is the wrong attitude. Never neglect a subject because you find it boring or difficult. These are the subjects in which you should be working your hardest. Your goal should be to make A's in all of your courses, not just the ones you like. If you let a boring course go for too long, you may get so far behind that you can never catch up. This will only make matters worse, and you may even fail the course. Always try to be a well-rounded person in everything you do!

How to Study

When you sit down to study, you should be willing to study very hard. If there is something else that you need to do before studying, then get it out of the way first. But you should never put off studying because you dislike a subject, or because you feel lazy. You are going to have to do the work sooner or later, so you might as well get it out of the way. What is required is the self-discipline to do what you have to do, whether you like it or not!

When you actually start to study you should "throw

yourself" into your work, and not let anything else interfere. This means that you will need the energy, enthusiasm, and determination to get your work done. To make the best use of your time, start working as soon as you sit down to study. If you are having a hard time getting into your studies, start off with something easy and then build up to the more difficult work. Sometimes students put off studying because they keep thinking about how difficult it will be. When they get started, it is often easier than they thought.

People who get the most done have the power of concentration. When you are studying, concentrate only on the subject at hand, and block everything else out of your mind. You really should not try to do two or more things at the same time, because you will do none of them very well. So don't try to watch television, play video games, or carry on a conversation with your friends while you are studying!

I think you will find that you can accomplish more if you study for long periods of time rather than short ones. Weekends are a good time to study, because you can put in a lot of time without interruptions. When you study continuously, you do not have to keep going back to review where you left off the last time. You will also be able to relate ideas more effectively because they are still fresh in your mind. Never study for so long, however, that you feel like you are getting worn out or bored.

When you are studying for long periods of time, be sure to allow time for breaks. You should take breaks when you need a breather from one subject, or when you are shifting over to another subject. I think it is a good idea to take a five- or ten-minute break every hour, but don't take so many—or make them so long—that they get in the way. During your break, you could do some chores around the house, listen to the radio, or just relax and do nothing. Do whatever *you* like so you can come back to your studies feeling refreshed and ready to go.

If you have been studying hard for most of the day, it is important to leave time to wind down. Don't study all the way up to when you are ready to go to bed. You will probably be too wound up to fall asleep. Take time to relax and do something fun, such as talking to a friend, reading a good novel, or watching a favorite show or program. You might even spend some time getting things ready for school the next day, so you won't have to hurry so much in the morning.

The key to having good study habits is to *practice good habits* in general. I firmly believe that you will be a better student if you are healthy. Always get plenty of rest. It is very difficult to concentrate if you are tired or have a headache. It is also important to eat properly. This means eating three good meals a day—including breakfast!—and staying away from too much junk food. You won't be able to work hard at your studies if you don't have any energy. This is the same advice that I give to my baseball players—eat right and get plenty of sleep if you want to play your best!

You will also be a better student if you are physically fit. You spend a lot of time sitting in school, so it is important to get up and move around afterwards. Kids usually get more exercise than adults because they have physical education at school. You might want to add to this by joining a team in your favorite sport. There are things you can do around the house on your own, such as a regular exercise program. You can also do things with your parents, such as throwing a ball around. Remember—if you are fit physically, you will perform better mentally!

The other side of the good-habits coin is *avoiding bad habits*. Although I know you have heard this a thousand times or more, it doesn't hurt to remind you again. Avoid taking harmful substances into your body, such as tobacco, alcohol, and drugs. They will prevent you from performing your best as a student, and may get you into much more serious trouble.

Sometimes activities become bad habits when we do them for too long. For example, there is nothing wrong with watching your favorite television program each day. On the other hand, if you spend several hours a day watching television, this leaves a lot less time for studying. Playing video games, listening to music, watching movies, or playing with friends are other good examples; it's okay to do these things as long as they do not get out of hand and interfere with your studies.

The simple fact is that most people, both adults and kids, are not very efficient in how they use their time. To become more efficient, you could practice something called "time management," which is an approach to using your time better.

Take a close look at how you spend an average school day. Make some notes on what you did when you got home from school that day. Did you start studying right away, or did you just goof off for a while? When you finally did start studying, did you make the best use of your time, or let other things get in your way? Now think about how you might have done some things differently. I'll bet you could have freed up a lot more time for studying—and still have had plenty of time left over for leisure activities!

If you haven't been using your time wisely, then you should probably make some changes in your schedule. It is very difficult to make big changes all at once, so you might start with making some small changes. After a while you can add some more changes, and before you know it you will have a better way of getting things done. Once you get things in order, you will find that you can get more work done in a shorter time.

As you think about using your time more wisely, I want to warn you about one thing: Don't spend so much time studying that you have no time left for anything else. You can overdo studying, just like you can do too much of anything else in life. Your goal should be to study enough to get A's in all of your classes, and still finish up in time to do all of the other things you want to do. It is possible to have it all!

You will find that the people who are the best at what they do—whatever it is—have a special way of approaching life. Successful people are focused, goal oriented, and hard working. This is true whether a person is a doctor, lawyer, scientist, professional athlete, business person, school teacher, or has any other occupation. The same is true for students. Develop the right study habits now, and you will not only be a good student, you will be better at the job you do when you get out of school!

RECAP

Studying will be much easier, more rewarding, and more fun, too, if you:

1. know when, where, what, and how to study,

2. practice good habits and avoid bad ones.

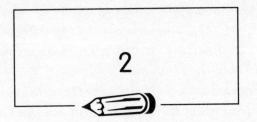

Conclusion

(. . . you're coming down the home stretch!)

In the first chapter you met Gary, the student who was everybody's choice for "Most Likely to Succeed" in the school yearbook. He was the straight-A student who played a different sport every season, and who was very active in extracurricular activities. Now I want you to meet Sarah. She is very similar to Gary, in that she also is a straight-A student, plays a different sport every season, and participates in a lot of activities after school.

Sarah has a tremendous amount of energy and likes being active all of the time. She plays softball in the spring, tennis in the summer, soccer in the fall, and basketball in the winter. Sarah is a member of the honor society and also participates in a number of activities at school, such as the drama, foreign language, music, and travel clubs. Because Sarah is involved in so many ac-

tivities, she knows just about everyone in school. She is also very outgoing and enjoys working with people. Her friends talked her into running for class president, and she easily won the election.

How does Sarah do it all? Like Gary, that is the same question that all of the teachers and students ask about Sarah. She is busy practically every minute of the day, but all the activity and excitement seem more like fun than work to her. Sarah likes her life so much that she wouldn't have it any other way. Anything less would be boring. She has set very high goals for herself, and gets enormous enjoyment from accomplishing them.

Sarah does have a secret for her success, and I would not be telling you the whole story without revealing it to you. By now you should have figured out the secret for yourself, because it was present in every other student you met in this book.

Whether Sarah is working in the classroom, playing on the athletic field, or participating in other activities at school, she applies all of the things discussed in this book to all her pursuits. She understands and practices the basic skills, and knows what she wants to accomplish. She works well with her teachers and coaches, never misses a class or a practice, works her hardest when she is there, and prepares ahead of time for everything. She is testwise in the classroom and razor-sharp on the athletic field, and she has the discipline and study habits that help her to become better every day. Sarah has her own high standards in all of her activities, and will not settle for anything less!

.　.　.

I have told you everything I know about how to become a straight-A student. You have learned several important skills that will help you to perform at the highest level in school. I have shown you how to read and get the most from books, how to take different types of tests and score highly on them, and how to prepare papers that are fun to write and interesting to read. I have also presented an entire system that shows you how to take the right subjects, prepare homework assignments, study for tests, and make the highest grades on tests. Finally, I have shown you how to develop good study habits so you can get all of your work done on time, and still have time left over to do other activities.

It is not enough to know something, however—you have to practice it. For example, you could learn everything there is to know about how to play the piano, but if you don't practice, then you will never be able to play very well. It is the same with school.

If you want to become a top student and make my system work for you, then you have to follow it. You will need to follow each of the steps I have described, not just occasionally, but throughout the entire year. If you do anything less than this, then you are not really following my system, and you will not get the best results.

I have worked with many students over the years, and I know from past experience what works the best. If you follow all of my steps all of the time you will see the greatest improvement, but if you follow only some of my steps only some of the time you may see little or even no progress.

Even though you have learned the best way to study and prepare for tests, you still need to work very hard to do well on them. Hard work is the only true road to success. The American inventor Thomas Edison, one of the greatest geniuses of all time probably said it best: "Genius is one percent inspiration and ninety-nine percent perspiration." In other words, it's not enough to be smart; you have to work very hard to succeed.

In order to work very hard, you need to be motivated. You must have the energy and drive to follow through with your actions. In order to be motivated, you need to be interested in what you are doing, feel that it is important, and have the energy and ambition to work very hard to achieve your goals. When you are motivated you always do your best, are unwilling to settle for anything less, and keep trying no matter how difficult the situation!

The main reason students have trouble getting motivated about school is that they think they would rather be doing something else. They often say, "If only I could get out of school, I wouldn't have to do any homework, and I could get a job and make some money." Then, when they get out into the working world later on, they often find that work is a bigger grind than school. Think of the situation in the following way: You are going to be in school for a certain amount of time anyway, so you might as well work hard and put forth your best effort!

If you make good grades in school, this will help you get into a good college, and obtain a good job later on. If you don't have a good education, you may end up with a boring job in which you have to work very hard and don't make much money.

Here is a final exercise to keep you motivated. Take out a sheet of paper and write down your goals in life. List very specific things, such as the type of job you want to get, where you want to live, and even how much money you want to make. Then think about what you need to do to accomplish these goals. I'll bet that getting a good education is part of it. Put this sheet of paper away and look at it from time to time, especially when you are feeling unmotivated. Just remind yourself that all of the hard work is for *you*.

It is also important for you to recognize that it is impossible to accomplish all of your goals immediately. Even if you are following everything I have laid out in this book, it will probably take a while for you to become a straight-A student. The more we work at anything in life, the better we become, and school is no exception. It takes time to develop good study habits and the skills needed to perform at the highest level in school. As you follow my study methods, you will start to see some improvement in your grades, and this, by itself, should give you some satisfaction. You should concentrate on what you need to do to become a straight-A student, rather than expecting to become one immediately!

You should also realize that even if you have worked your very hardest in school and done everything necessary, it is impossible to be perfect. We are all human beings, and we are going to make some mistakes and have some disappointments. Don't let these upset you. If you are following my study system, you should start to see some real progress right away, and you will do even better in the future because you are on the right track. You will also get more enjoyment out of your schoolwork, because we all like things that we do well. A certain feeling of pride comes from being a good student.

What can you expect to get for all of your efforts? Researchers have found that people who do well in school are more likely to have success in other parts of their lives. Good students are more likely to have friends, participate in extracurricular activities, and hold school offices. They are also more likely to be successful when they get out of school, in terms of getting better jobs and having a more comfortable standard of living. More broadly, a good education influences just about every part of your life. A real sense of satisfaction comes from obtaining knowledge and understanding how the world works. In summary, a good education makes you a more complete person.

Well, we have come to the end of a long, but, I hope, enjoyable journey. The coach is ready to get you out on the academic playing field. You now know what your mission is—to become a straight-A student!—and how to accomplish it. Many people have told me that they wish they had known the things in this book when they were younger, because school would have been more fun and rewarding.

I wish you great success in your studies, and invite you to tell me about your accomplishments. You can reach me through my publisher, whose address is listed in the front of the book.

I will leave you with one last thought to guide you

on your journey; it comes from Robert Louis Stevenson, the author of *Treasure Island*, and if you follow it you will certainly find treasure in your life. It is my favorite saying, because it describes what life is all about:

RECAP

"To be what we are, and to become what we are capable of becoming, is the only end of life."

—Robert Louis Stevenson

WHAT YOU HAVE LEARNED

3. Making It Work for You

(. . . by working smarter, not harder!)

RULE 1

Develop good study habits and follow them regularly if you want to become a straight-A student.

RULE 2

"To be what we are, and to become what we are capable of becoming, is the only end of life."

—Robert Louis Stevenson

ABOUT THE AUTHOR

Dr. Gordon W. Green, Jr., is well known as an author in the field of education. His first book, *Getting Straight A's* (1985), has over three hundred thousand copies in print, has been translated into Spanish and Polish, and was advertised for many years in *Parade* magazine. His other books on education include *Helping Your Child to Learn* (1994), and *Helping Your Child to Learn Math* (1995). Dr. Green has also written a book for people at work, titled *Getting Ahead at Work* (1989).

Dr. Green bases his writings in education on his own personal experience and work with students at all age levels. During his studies toward a Ph.D. in economics from The George Washington University in 1984, Dr. Green received an A in every course he took. He was able to do this while working full-time at his regular job, and taking care of home and family responsibilities at the same time. Dr. Green attributes his success to his unique system of study, which he has adapted for younger students in this book. He has helped students improve their performance at all levels, including elementary, middle, high school, and college. Dr. Green travels to different schools to teach his study methods, and has spent a lot of time working with college athletes, especially baseball players.

When he is not writing books, working with students, or coaching baseball, Dr. Green works full-time for the U.S. Census Bureau. He is a member of the Senior Executive Service and Chief of the Governments Division at the Census Bureau. His office issues a wide range of financial and employment information for governments and educational institutions at all levels. Before working in this capacity, Dr. Green was for many years in charge of the preparation of the nation's official statistics on income and poverty. His work in connection with the Census Bureau is widely published in magazines and professional journals. Dr. Green has also served as the chair of the National Forum on Education Statistics, and continues to be an active member.

Dr. Green lives with his wife, Maureen, and his three children, Heidi, Dana, and Christopher, in Fairfax Station, Virginia.

Index

academic program, 113–14
author's message,
    understanding when
    reading, 41–43

books
    previewing before reading, 35–
    37
    reading at own pace, 43–45
books (reading), 31–46
    continually asking questions,
    37–39
    getting ready, 34–35
    looking up new words in
    dictionary, 40–41
    previewing the book, 35–37
    reading at own pace, 43–45
    recap, 46
    understanding author's
    message, 41–43

class (missing and tardiness),
    125–31
    creating a bad impression,
    128
    and the grading period, 130
    importance of not missing,
    21
    missing important
    information, 128
    recap, 131

test questions and class
    lectures, 128–29, 130
class (sitting up front), 123–37
    better prepared to answer
    questions, 135
    hearing better, 136
    impressing the teacher, 136
    less distractions, 136
    recap, 137
computer science
    as a subject choice, 116–17

dictionary
    looking up new words in, 40–
    41
distribution system (grades on a
    "curve"), 185–86

Edison, Thomas, 158
electives, choosing to take, 117
English as a subject choice, 115–
    16
essay exams, 51–60

final exams (showing what you
    do), 189–94
    knowing what material will
    be covered, 191
    looking for major themes, 192–
    93
    recap, 194

final exams (*continued*)
  reviewing previous exams,
    193
  showing teacher what you
    have learned, 191
  start studying well ahead of
    time, 192
  See also tests
first draft (of paper), 96–98
  beginning or introduction, 96
  ending or conclusion, 98
  middle or body, 96–98

general programs, 113
getting ready to read, 34–35
getting started, 15–23
  believing in yourself, 17
  knowing what you're doing,
    17–18
  recap, 23
  taking school seriously, 17
guidance counselors
  and subject choice, 114

homework (completing before
    class), 139–47
  asking and answering good
    questions, 143, 146
  being prepared for the next
    class, 143
  different types of, 141
  outlines, 141–42
  reading all listed books, 142
  recap, 147
  turning in assignments on
    time, 145
  understanding more of the
    lecture, 143
how to study, 205–9

mathematics as a subject
    choice, 116

notes (reviewing), 159–65
  adding headings, 162

clearing up inconsistencies
    with teacher, 162, 163
  filling in missing information
    and abbreviations, 162
  organizing your notes, 162
  recap, 165
  rethinking, 162
  reviewing notes as starting to
    study for test, 163
  rewriting, 161–62
notes (taking during class), 149–
    58
  detailed notes, 154
  importance of supplies, 154
  listening carefully, 151–52,
    153
  looking for potential exam
    questions, 156
  neat notebooks, importance
    of, 156
  questioning teacher's
    mistakes, 152–53
  recap, 158
  trusting your memory, 157
  use abbreviations, 154–55
  white space, importance of,
    155–56
  write everything of
    importance, 154

objective exams, 61–63
open-book exams, 69–70
oral exams and reports, 72–77

papers (first draft of), 96–98
  beginning or introduction, 96
  ending or conclusion, 98
  middle or body, 96–98
papers (how to write), 83–102
  asking specific questions, 89–
    90
  developing an outline, 94
  final form, 99–100
  first draft, 96–98
  good writing, 20

picking a good subject, 88–89
research, 90–94
starting early, 100–101
physical education, choosing to
    take, 117
problem exams, 63–69

questions
    continually asking when
        reading, 37–39

reading a book, 31–46
    continually asking questions,
        37–39
    getting ready, 34–35
    looking up new words in
        dictionary, 40–41
    previewing the book, 35–37
    reading at own pace, 43–45
    recap, 46
    understanding author's
        message, 41–43
recaps
    being testwise and confident,
        187
    completing homework before
        class, 147
    final exams, 194
    getting started, 23
    never missing class, 131
    preparing for tests ahead of
        time, 177
    reading a book, 46
    reviewing notes, 165
    sitting up front in class, 137
    study habits, 210
    taking notes during class, 158
    taking tests, 82
    taking the right subjects, 118
    working with teachers, 124
    writing a paper, 102

setting goals, 20–21
skills you need, 27–29
    reading a book, 31–46

review, 103
taking a test
writing a paper
Stevenson, Robert Lewis, 217,
    218
study habits, 199–210
    how to study, 205–9
    recap, 210
    what to study, 204–5
    when to study, 201–3
    where to study, 203
subjects (making the right
        choice), 111–18
    computer science, 116–17
    electives, 117
    English, 115–16
    guidance counselors and, 114
    mathematics, 116
    physical education, 117
    taking courses in right order,
        114–18
    taking the academic program,
        113–14
    recap, 118
supplies
    and note taking, 154
    and tests, 50

take-home exams, 71–72
teachers (working with), 119–
    24
    getting interested in their
        subject, 123
    knowing their likes and
        dislikes, 123–24
    learning their style in the
        classroom, 123
    making a good impression on,
        importance of, 21
    recap, 124
    thinking of as coaches, 121–
        22
technical programs, 113
tests, 47–82
    being prepared, 50–51

tests (*continued*)
  cheating, 80–81
  facing up to, 19–20
  recap, 82
  reviewing answers, 79–81
  using time wisely, 80
  writing clearly, 78–79
  See also final exams
tests (different types of)
  essay exams, 51–60
  objective exams, 61–63
  open-book exams, 69–70
  oral exams and reports, 72–77
  problem exams, 63–69
  take-home exams, 71–72
tests (preparations for taking)
  arriving on time, 50
  listening to classmates prior to test, 50
  reading and listening to instructions, 50–51
  supplies, 50
  writing name on test paper, 51
tests (preparing for ahead of time), 167–77
  equations, graphs, and charts, rewriting, 174
  materials teacher hands out, paying attention to, 174–75
  memorizing information, 175

questions a teacher might ask, thinking about, 174
recap, 177
relating details, 172
reviewing in an organized manner, 171–72, 175–76
reviewing notes at least three times, 171–73
studying at the last minute, 176
studying in advance, 171
testwise and confident (becoming), 179–87
  applying what you know, 186–87
  believing in yourself, 182–84
  the distribution system (grades on a "curve"), 185–86
  fear of failure, 183–84
  keeping an open mind, 181–82
  knowing your teacher's style, 185–86
  recap, 187
  reviewing wrong answers, 184–85
Twain, Mark, 142

what to study, 204–5
what you have learned, 218
  10 rules, 195–96
when to study, 201–3
where to study, 203